A MAN
FRENCH PROSE
FOR ADVANCE

A Manual of French Prose Composition for Advanced Students

J. C. IRESON M.A. (LONDON) DOCTEUR ÈS LETTRES
Professor of French in the University of Hull

with references to
A GRAMMAR OF PRESENT-DAY FRENCH
by J. E. MANSION

HARRAP LONDON

First published in Great Britain 1961
by George G. Harrap & Co. Ltd
182–184 High Holborn, London WC1V 7AX
Reprinted: 1966; 1970; 1971; 1976; 1977

ISBN 0 245 52982 9

Printed in Great Britain by
Biddles Ltd, Guildford, Surrey

PREFACE

It is by now unnecessary to justify prose composition either as a means of learning to write a modern language or as an intellectual discipline. The exercise has long established itself in sixth form and university courses. If it is necessary to justify the publication of yet another collection of passages for translation into French, I need perhaps do no more than indicate the scarcity of books giving a large choice of pieces from contemporary writers, a scarcity which this book is designed to remedy. By far the greater number of the extracts I have chosen are examples of modern English, with a few passages, chiefly in the more advanced sections, taken from writers of earlier periods.

Generally speaking, I have tried to keep to the tradition already established by a number of excellent manuals. These have amply demonstrated the value of French prose composition as a rigorous and delicate operation calling for literary perception as well as linguistic flair and fullness. It was perhaps inevitable that the majority of such manuals, particularly those which abstracted and organised linguistic points involved in the translation of the passages, should deal mostly with pieces of English accredited and well established. But it is now unrealistic, in view of the rapid accretion and change which characterise both English and French, to insist on composition as a formal rendering of a settled and probably outdated style. I am, on the other hand, aware of the risk involved in collecting contemporaneous passages which, however apposite at the moment, may become, in a short while, merely untopical and lacking in general interest. This is a risk which has to be taken when the decision is made, as here, to range widely over modern subjects and styles. Some users of the book may indeed think that I have at times gone too far towards technical jargon, officialese, or Americanisms. This is a question of opinion. My constant effort has been, as far as possible, to select pieces for their literary value, as well as for the linguistic tests they contain.

I have not attempted to write a preamble on points of translation, nor have I included any kind of glossary. The dangers of over-simplification and omission are obvious when the compass of such observations or lists is strictly limited. The inadequacies of a potted grammar are equally obvious. I have accordingly forborne to try to teach translation in a preface. Indeed, the range of the present *Harrap's Standard French and English Dictionary*, the number and excellence of the special dictionaries and works of reference that are readily available at the present time, underline the impracticability of such a venture. I have therefore assumed from the start that the students who work with this manual will be prepared to read widely among the existing authorities in their search for terms, equivalents and guarantees of usage, and I have supplied, as an introduction, a select list of such authorities with comments upon their particular value.

The pieces are arranged in four grades, marked by one, two, three or four asterisks. These grades are intended to cover the years between the senior half of the sixth form and the Final Honours stage of the universities. Students working for general degrees will, I think, find the first three grades suited to their purpose. There is, of course, nothing ultimate about such a grading. Teachers and students will be the best judges of their own requirements.

I have added notes to individual exercises. These are designed to diminish in number with the upward grading of the passages. No notes are given to passages marked by four asterisks. The purport of the notes is mainly grammatical. The majority of them are references to points dealt with in *A Grammar of Present-day French* by J. E. Mansion. They are intended to be reminders of matters which are common sources of error in the French written by students at about university entrance level. In other cases, I have suggested modifications of the English which may simplify individual phrases and constructions for translation purposes. I have not wished to remove the difficulties from the texts by suggesting French renderings which, however adequate, do not add to the active process of translation on the part of the student. The place for such renderings is in a parallel volume containing model translations. A Key giving proposed translations of the three- and four-star passages only is published separately and is available to teachers only, from Messrs. Harrap.

J. C. I.

ACKNOWLEDGMENTS

Our thanks are due to the following authors, publishers and literary representatives for permission to reproduce copyright material:

Messrs George Allen and Unwin, Ltd (*Human Knowledge, its Scope and Limits* by Bertrand Russell; *The Dilemma of our Times* by Professor Harold Laski); Mr Edmund Wilson and Messrs W. H. Allen, Ltd (*The Scrolls from the Dead Sea*); Messrs Edward Arnold, Ltd (*Aspects of the Novel* by E. M. Forster); the Editor of "Progress," the Magazine of the Unilever Group (*Strictly for Women* by Susan Hicklin); the University Press, Cambridge (*Art and Reality* by Joyce Cary; *Patterns of Discovery* by N. R. Hanson); Messrs Jonathan Cape, Ltd (*Horses and Men* by Sherwood Anderson; *Dubliners* by James Joyce; *The Mint* by T. E. Lawrence; *Sunlight on the Lawn* by Beverley Nichols; *Mortal Strife* by John Cowper Powys; *My Uncle Silas* by H. E. Bates); Miss Rebecca West and Messrs Jonathan Cape, Ltd (*The Strange Necessity*); Cassell and Co. Ltd (*The Second World War* by Sir Winston S. Churchill); Messrs Chatto and Windus, Ltd (*Elizabeth and Essex* by Lytton Strachey; *Flowers of the Forest* by David Garnett; *Sublime Tobacco* by Sir Compton Mackenzie; *The Perennial Philosophy*, *Antic Hay*, and *Brave New World Revisited* by Aldous Huxley; *The Common Pursuit* by F. R. Leavis; *The Uses of Literacy* by Richard Hoggart); Messrs William Collins, Sons and Co. Ltd (*English Cities and Small Towns* by John Betjeman in the "Britain in Pictures" series; *Keeping up Appearances*, and *The Towers of Trebizond* by Rose Macaulay; *The Whisper in the Gloom* by Nicholas Blake; *The Story of England* by Sir Arthur Bryant; *Mine Own Executioner* by Nigel Balchin; *Shakespeare* by Ivor Brown; *Dumb Witness* by Agatha Christie); Mr Ray Robinson and Messrs William Collins, Sons and Co. Ltd (*From the Boundary*); Field-Marshal the Viscount Montgomery of Alamein and Messrs William Collins, Sons and Co. Ltd (*Memoirs* of Lord Montgomery); Mr Paul Brickhill and Messrs William Collins, Sons and Co. Ltd (*Reach for the Sky*); Messrs Constable and Co. Ltd (*Springtime* by J. B. Morton; *That's Me All Over* by Cornelia Otis Skinner); The Cresset Press (*Fables* by Jacquetta Hawkes); Books for Pleasure, Ltd (*Christocracy* by J. Middleton Murry); Messrs André Deutsch, Ltd (*My Old Man's a Dustman* by Wolf Mankowitz; *Image of a Society* by Roy Fuller); Dennis Dobson (*Hang your Hat on a*

Pension by Matthew Finch); Messrs Eyre and Spottiswoode, Ltd (*Letters from Compton Deverell* by 'BB'; *A History of British Painting* by Ernest Short); Messrs Faber and Faber, Ltd (*Siegfried's Journey* and *Memoirs of a Fox-hunting Man* by Siegfried Sassoon; *The Lord of the Flies* by William Golding; *Plowmen's Clocks* by Alison Uttley; *So Much Love, So Little Money* by Lyn Irvine; *The Use of Poetry* by T. S. Eliot; *The Untutored Townsman's Invasion of the Country* by Professor C. E. M. Joad; *Strangers and Brothers* by Sir Charles Snow; *The Hidden Years* by Travers Otway; *Icon and Idea* by Sir Herbert Read); Mr Randall Jarrell, Messrs Alfred A. Knopf, Inc. and Messrs Faber and Faber, Ltd (*Pictures from an Institution*); Mr Henry Williamson and Messrs Faber and Faber, Ltd (*The Star-Born*); John Farquharson, Ltd (*The Tragic Muse* and *The Turn of the Screw* by Henry James); The Free Press of Glencoe, Illinois (*The Phenomenology of Moral Experience* by Professor Maurice Mandelbaum); Messrs Victor Gollancz Ltd (*The Outsider* by Colin Wilson; *Lucky Jim* by Kingsley Amis; *Mother and Son* by I. Compton-Burnett; *Personal Pleasures* by Rose Macaulay; *The Breaking Point* by Daphne du Maurier; *Clouds of Witness* by Dorothy L. Sayers); Mr Art Buchwald and Messrs Victor Gollancz, Ltd (*More Caviar*); Mr Michael Innes and Messrs Victor Gollancz, Ltd (*The Secret Vanguard*); Dr A. J. Cronin and Messrs Victor Gollancz, Ltd (*Shannon's Way*); The Editor of "The Guardian" (*Mr Attlee* by Harry Boardman); Messrs. Hamish Hamilton, Ltd (*Thurber Country* by James Thurber; *Inside Russia Today* by John Gunther); Rupert Hart-Davis, Ltd (*Beware of Children* by Verily Anderson; *All in Due Time* by Humphry House; *The Picture Season in London* by Henry James); Messrs William Heinemann, Ltd (*The Fortunes of Richard Mahoney* by Henry Handel Richardson; *Sweet Thursday* by John Steinbeck; *Letters to My Daughter* by the Baroness Summerskill; *Pnin* by Vladimir Nabokov; *Assignment to Catastrophe* by General Sir Edward Spears; *As It Happened* by the Earl Attlee; *Adam in Moonshine* and *Angel Pavement* by J. B. Priestley; *No Highway* and *Requiem for a Wren* by Nevil Shute); Mr W. Somerset Maugham and Messrs William Heinemann, Ltd (*Cakes and Ale* and *The Complete Short Stories of Somerset Maugham*); Mr Graham Greene and Messrs William Heinemann, Ltd (*The Heart of the Matter*); The Controller of Her Majesty's Stationery Office (*Roadcraft*, H.M. Stationery Office Manual, 1955); Mr Patrick Heron and the British Broadcasting Corporation (*Nicolas de Staël: 1914–1955* from "The Listener");

The Tweedsmuir Trustees and Messrs Hodder and Stoughton, Ltd (*The Three Hostages* by John Buchan); Mr Leonard Woolf and The Hogarth Press, Ltd (*The Waves* and *A Haunted House* by Virginia Woolf); Messrs Hutchinson and Co. Ltd (*The Physicist's Conception of Nature* by Werner Heisenberg; *One Hundred and Twenty-eight Witnesses* by R. H. Mottram); Miss Rebecca West and Messrs Hutchinson and Co. Ltd (*Harriet Hume*); Messrs Michael Joseph, Ltd (*Village School* by 'Miss Read'; *A Ship of the Line* by C. S. Forester; *Thursday Afternoons* by Monica Dickens; *On the Edge of the Sea* by F. L. Green; *To Be a Pilgrim* by Joyce Cary); Mr Raymond Postgate and Messrs Michael Joseph, Ltd (*The Ledger is Kept*); Mr Maurice Kennedy (*Vladivostok*); John Lane, the Bodley Head, Ltd (*Gladly Oddly* by Paul Jennings; *Musical Studies* by Ernest Newman; *Jobber Skald* by John Cowper Powys); Mr E. Lipson (*A Planned Economy or Free Enterprise*); Messrs Longmans, Green and Co. Ltd (*The Meaning of Beauty* by Eric Newton; *English Social History* by G. M. Trevelyan; *Power in Trade Unions* by V. L. Allen; *Politics in Post-War France* by Philip Williams); Mr Henry Williamson and Messrs Macdonald and Co. Ltd (*A Fox under my Cloak*); Mr P. F. Strawson and Messrs Macmillan and Co. Ltd (*The Revolution in Philosophy*); Miss Rebecca West and Messrs Macmillan and Co. Ltd (*The Meaning of Treason*); Messrs Macmillan and Co. Ltd (*The Travelling Woman* and *The Contenders* by John Wain; *Follow M'Leader* by Sir Osbert Sitwell; *The Portobello Road* by Muriel Spark; *The Satisfactory* by V. S. Pritchett; *The Genius* by Frank O'Connor); the executors of the late Sir Rider Haggard (*Allan Quatermain*); Messrs Methuen and Co. Ltd (*Blue Days at Sea* by H. V. Morton; *The Writer's Trade* by L. A. G. Strong; *On Fighting against Odds* from *Visibility Good* by E. V Lucas; *France: the Fourth Republic* by Dorothy Pickles; *First and Last* by Hilaire Belloc); Messrs John Murray, Ltd (*Landscape into Art* by Sir Kenneth Clark); The Public Trustee (*Ancient Lights* from *Ten Minute Stories* by Algernon Blackwood); the executors of the late H. G. Wells (*The Food of the Gods*); Odhams Press, Ltd (*The Bridge* by Howard Maier; *The Explosion* by John Pudney); The Oxford University Press (*Some Thoughts on Beethoven's Choral Symphony* by Dr Ralph Vaughan Williams; *The Chequer'd Shade* by John Press; *The Allegory of Love* by Professor C. S. Lewis; *Civilisation on Trial* by Arnold Toynbee; *Principles of Social and Political Theory* by Sir Ernest Barker); the Cecil Gray Trustees (*Contingencies and Other Essays*); Messrs Penguin Books, Ltd (*An Outline of European

Architecture by Professor Nikolaus Pevsner; *Jazz* by Rex Harris; *Architecture: 19th and 20th Centuries* by H. R. Hitchcock in the "Pelican History of Art"; *The Case for Conservatism* by the Viscount Hailsham; *Tudor England* by S. T. Bindoff in the "Pelican History of England"; Messrs Putnam and Co. Ltd (*Saturday Afternoon* by Dorothy Whipple); Messrs Routledge and Kegan Paul Ltd (*Places of the Mind* by Geoffrey Grigson); Mr Christopher Salmon (*Broadcasting, Speech and Writing*); Messrs Charles Scribner's Sons (*Tender is the Night* and *The Great Gatsby* by F. Scott Fitzgerald, © 1926, Charles Scribner's Sons; © 1953, Frances Scott Fitzgerald Lanahan); Messrs Martin Secker and Warburg, Ltd (*Hurry on Down* by John Wain; *South Wind* by Norman Douglas; *The Road to Wigan Pier* by George Orwell); The Literary Trustees of Walter de la Mare and The Society of Authors (*Early One Morning* and *The Almond Tree*); The Society of Authors and Miss Rosamund Lehmann (*A Note in Music*); The Times Publishing Co. Ltd (*Double Claim, Defence and The Bomb, The French Assembly Reduced to a Debating Society, Zeta to Icse* reprinted from "The Times"; *The Moral Anarchists* reprinted from "The Times Literary Supplement").

BIBLIOGRAPHY

A. WORKS SUGGESTED FOR CONSTANT REFERENCE

ed. J. E. MANSION, *Harrap's Standard French and English Dictionary*, vol. I, French-English; vol. II, English-French; *Supplement*, edited by R. P. L. Ledésert, 1961.

Indispensable for all advanced work.

J. E. MANSION, *A Grammar of Present-day French* (Harrap, new edition, 1952).

N.B. The footnotes to passages given in the pages which follow refer frequently to this grammar. For systematic revision, an edition with exercises is available.

B. DICTIONARIES OF THE FRENCH LANGUAGE

Dictionnaire de l'Académie française (Hachette, 8e édition, 1932–5).

E. LITTRÉ, *Dictionnaire de la Langue française* (Hachette, 1863–73). *Supplément*, 1877

The two main authorities. Littré's work is more complex and more fully stocked with examples. The *Dictionnaire de L'Académie* is clearly arranged, though in some respects is less exhaustive than Littré. The dates indicate the limits of each dictionary.

P. ROBERT, *Dictionnaire alphabétique et analogique de la Langue française* (Société du nouveau Littré, 1951 *ff.*).

A. HATZFELD, A. DARMESTETER, A. THOMAS, *Dictionnaire générale de la Langue française* (Delagrave, 1920).

An excellent shorter dictionary. Treats the main sense only of the words given.

C. OTHER DICTIONARIES

Grand Larousse encyclopédique (1960 *ff.*).

Petit Larousse (1959).

Dictionnaire usuel, Quillet Flammarion (Harrap, 1963).

The best encyclopaedic dictionaries available. Remarkably up-to-date.

R. Bailly, *Dictionnaire des Synonymes de la Langue française* (Larousse, 1947).

H. Bénac, *Dictionnaire des Synonymes* (Hachette, 1956).

These attempt to fix the shades of meaning which differentiate terms whose general sense is roughly the same. Useful for narrowing down the search for the precise word to fit a particular context.

C. Maquet, *Dictionnaire analogique* (Larousse, 1936).
Useful as an aid to the hunting down of the exact term. The operation involved supposes a fair knowledge of French.

J. G. Anderson, *Le Mot juste* (Dent, 1932).
Revised by L. C. Harmer, 1938.
Succinct. Specifically prepared for English-speaking users. Most useful at about university entrance level.

Kettridge's Technical Dictionary (Routledge, 1947), vol. I, French-English; vol. II, English-French.

Kettridge's French-English and English-French Dictionary of Commercial and Financial terms, Phrases and Practice (Routledge, 1946).

The Oxford English Dictionary.

H. W. Fowler, *A Dictionary of Modern English Usage* (Oxford, 1926); 2nd ed. 1965

D. Other works

Grammaire du XXe Siècle : Traité complet de la Langue française (Larousse, 1936).

M. Grevisse, *Le bon Usage* (Gembloux: Editions J. Duculot; Paris: Geuthner, 7e édition, 1959).
An indispensable work of reference where subtle or difficult points of grammar and syntax are involved. Detailed and lengthy, but excellently indexed.

R. Georgin, *Finesses et Difficultés de notre Langue* (André Bonne, 1952).

J. Marouzeau, *Précis de Stylistique française* (Masson, 3e édition, 1950).

L. C. Harmer, *The French Language Today* (Hutchinson's University Library, 1954).

These three works call for systematic study. It is not always easy to consult them on precise points.

J.-P. Vinay and J. Darbelnet, *Stylistique comparée du français et de l'anglais* (Harrap, 1958).

An excellent manual for the translator working with modern French and English. The examples are valuable, but the indexing is not detailed, which makes it a work to study systematically rather than one to consult on precise points. The attention of students could profitably be drawn to the translations of English texts (Appendice III, textes III, IV, V, VI, VII).

C. H. Bissell, *Prepositions in French and English* (Richard R. Smith, New York, 1947).

A lengthy work on one of the most difficult aspects of English-French translation. Carefully categorised, but lacks a detailed index, which often makes rapid consultation difficult.

F. Boillot, *Le second vrai Ami du Traducteur anglais-français et français-anglais* (Oliven, 1956).

The first edition, *Le vrai ami du Traducteur* (P.U.F.), appeared in 1930.

Helpful, alphabetic, lively. Deals with translation problems raised by homonyms.

NOTE

The paragraph numbers in the notes to passages refer to *A Grammar of Present-day French*, by J. E. Mansion

CONTENTS

SECTION I: NARRATIVE

SECTION II: DESCRIPTIVE

SECTION III: CRITICISM

SECTION IV: CONVERSATIONAL

SECTION V: HISTORICAL AND POLITICAL

SECTION VI: CHARACTERS AND PORTRAITS

SECTION VII: REFLECTIVE AND PHILOSOPHICAL

SECTION VIII: MISCELLANEOUS PASSAGES DEALING WITH MODERN LIFE AND THOUGHT

NARRATIVE

I

*RIFLE PRACTICE***

On the lawn below his window, about where the stake had stood yesterday morning, was set a plain kitchen chair, and on this chair was sitting the old woman who called herself Nanny. Her back was towards him, and she was either asleep or admiring the view. Bert stayed at the window, not in any positive hope of seeing other human figures—indeed, he had not even bothered to put on his spectacles—but as[1] a castaway surveys the expanses of ocean, in a dreary self-hypnosis, and because there is nothing else to look at.

Presently, he heard the sound of a window being gently opened, below him and to his right. The muzzle of the rifle poked out. It was trained in the same direction as yesterday. Bert opened his mouth, yelling a warning to the old woman asleep on the kitchen chair. His cry was drowned by the crack of the rifle, to which, like an almost instantaneous echo, was added a sort of sharp 'clock'—the sound of a cricket bat meeting a ball—and the head of the figure seated in the chair visibly jerked.

Bert scrambled back to bed, hid his face in the pillow; then, as further shots followed, he dug his fingers into his ears, sobbing. The memory of another shot, another head jerking and disintegrating, in[2] the derelict house, rushed back at him. The old woman was silly, aggravating; but she had been kind to him. Now, for all he knew, he would be alone in this mansion with the person who had killed her. But why had she been killed? It seemed crazy, a piece of mad, meaningless nightmare. Then Bert remembered the letter he had written. Perhaps she really had tried to post it, and been caught, and this was her punishment.

Bert was still sobbing, hiccoughing with sobs, when he heard a key turn in the lock. He burrowed under the clothes, away[3] from whoever was coming in. A hand pulled the bedclothes back. A voice said, "Now, now, Master Bert. Hiding?"

It was Nanny.

NICHOLAS BLAKE:

The Whisper in the Gloom (Collins, 1954)

[1] "In the same way as."

[2] Connect "shot" and "head" with "in the derelict house," by inserting a phrase or phrases.

[3] Use a verb.

2

*RUNNING WITH THE HARE AND HUNTING WITH THE HOUNDS*****

Ill-feeling increased. Those long, lovely Sunday rounds of beer and cheese, and wind-on-the-heath-brother, became things of a remote and kindly past. Chaffers and Flyte-Foller met now never of their own choice. And seldom by accident, for the literary hostesses of that day knew their ground, to which they perpetually kept their ears, and were careful not to invite the rivals at the same time to the same house.

Poor Owen, gone were his outings! No longer could he preen himself within the nimbus of the dual glory. Each great man had forbidden in his presence the very mention of the other's name. . . . Notwithstanding, he continued faithful to them both in his own fashion.

Matrimony further envenomed their new hatred: since, as it chanced, they were married on the same day; with the consequence that each obtained only half of the half-column in the press which, under other circumstances, would have been consecrated to him alone. Besides, they separately, but in identical terms, complained to Owen, it cheapened the whole institution. (Owen, in order to maintain a balance, felt himself obliged to attend the marriage of one, and bridal reception of the other.) Their wives, too, took on, with the weddings, their share of the growing feud. Toque challenged toque, blouse dared blouse, feather-boa defied feather-boa and bolero outbid bolero. Fortunately they differed considerably in their appearance: Phoebe Flyte-Foller was tall, dark and mournful, with long ear-rings a-dangle from sad ears, while Violet Chaffers was short, golden-haired, a gay *vivandière*, with the foam of Roedean still clinging to her hockey-stick; yet, the very first time they saw each other—at a large evening party—they were dressed alike!

SIR OSBERT SITWELL:

"Follow M'Leader" from *Winter's Tales I* (Macmillan, 1955)

3

*DREAM DANCE**

Some dreams[1] I have had in this cottage seem to give strength to the opinion that there is a psychic memory attached to certain neighbourhoods.

Last night, after walking in a dream among buildings with strangely intense light on them, I heard a faint rhythm of music beginning far away on some stringed instrument.

It came closer to me, gradually increasing in quickness and volume with an irresistibly definite progression. When it was quite near the sound began to move on my nerves and blood, and to urge me to dance with them.

I knew that if I yielded[2] I would be carried away to some moment of terrible agony, so I struggled to remain quiet, holding my knees together with[3] my hands.

The music increased continually, sounding like the strings of harps, tuned to a forgotten scale, and having a resonance as searching as the strings of the 'cello.

Then the luring excitement became more powerful than my will, and my limbs moved in spite of me.

In a moment I was swept away by a whirlwind of notes. My breath and my thoughts and every impulse of my body became a form of the dance, till I could not distinguish between the instruments and the rhythm and my own person or consciousness.

For a while it seemed an excitement that was filled with joy; then it grew into an ecstasy where all existence was lost in a vortex of movement. I could not think there had ever been a life beyond the whirling of the dance.

Then with a shock the ecstasy turned to an agony and rage. I struggled to free myself, but seemed only to increase the passion of the steps I moved to. When I shrieked I could only echo the notes of the rhythm.

At last, with a movement of uncontrollable frenzy, I broke back to consciousness and awoke.

I dragged myself trembling to the window of the cottage and looked out. The moon was glittering across the bay, and there was no sound anywhere on the island.

J. M. SYNGE:
The Aran Islands

[1] Insert a relative pronoun.
[2] § **229**. (*a*). [3] § **287**. *Notes*. 1.

4

*AN AFTER-DINNER SPEECH**

The raisins and almonds and figs and apples and oranges and chocolates and sweets were now passed about the table, and Aunt Julia invited all the guests to have either port or sherry. At first Mr Bartell D'Arcy refused to take either, but one of his neighbours nudged him and whispered something to him, upon which he allowed his glass to be filled. Gradually as the last glasses were being filled the conversation ceased. A pause followed, broken only by the noise of the wine and by unsettlings of chairs. The Misses Morkan, all three, looked down at the table-cloth. Someone coughed once or twice, and then a few gentlemen patted the table gently as a signal for silence. The silence came and Gabriel pushed back his chair and stood up.

The patting at once grew louder in encouragement and then ceased altogether. Gabriel leaned his ten trembling fingers on the table-cloth and smiled nervously at the company. Meeting a row of upturned faces he raised his eyes to the chandelier. The piano was playing a waltz tune and he could hear the skirts sweeping against the drawing-room door. People, perhaps, were standing in the snow on the quay outside, gazing up at the lighted windows and listening to the waltz music. The air was pure there. In the distance lay the park, where the trees were weighted with snow. The Wellington Monument wore a gleaming cap of snow that flashed westward over the white field of Fifteen Acres.

He began:

"Ladies and Gentlemen,

It has fallen to my lot this evening, as in years past, to perform a very pleasing task, but a task for which I am afraid my poor powers as a speaker are all too inadequate."

JAMES JOYCE:

"The Dead" from *Dubliners* (Richards, 1914)

5

*ON THE RIVIERA*****

At the hotel the girl made the reservation in idiomatic but rather flat French, like something remembered. When they were installed on the ground floor she walked into the glare of the french windows and out a few steps on to the stone veranda that ran the length of the hotel. When she walked she carried herself like a ballet-dancer, not slumped down on her hips but held up in the small of her back. Out there the hot light clipped close her shadow and she retreated—it was too bright to see. Fifty yards away the Mediterranean yielded up its pigments, moment by moment, to the brutal sunshine; below the balustrade a faded Buick cooked on the hotel drive.

Indeed, of all the region only the beach stirred with activity. Three British nannies sat knitting the slow pattern of Victorian England, the pattern of the forties, the sixties, and the eighties, into sweaters and socks, to the tune of gossip as formalised as incantation; closer to the sea a dozen persons kept house under striped umbrellas, while their dozen children pursued unintimidated fish through the shallows or lay naked and glistening with coconut oil out in the sun.

As Rosemary came on to the beach a boy of twelve ran past her and dashed into the sea with exultant cries. Feeling the impactive scrutiny of strange faces, she took off her bathrobe and followed. She floated face down for a few yards and, finding it shallow, staggered to her feet and plodded forward, dragging slim legs like weights against the resistance of the water. When it was about breast high, she glanced back toward shore: a bald man in a monocle and a pair of tights, his tufted chest thrown out, his brash navel sucked in, was regarding her attentively. As Rosemary returned the gaze the man dislodged the monocle, which went into hiding amid the facetious whiskers of his chest, and poured himself a glass of something from a bottle in his hand.

F. Scott Fitzgerald:
Tender is the Night (Chatto and Windus, 1934)

6

*CLIMBING A LADDER***

He had always been afraid of heights and climbing, and for a man of his moderate size and weight he was clumsy. Being afraid, he kept his body in too close to the ladder, so that there was no room for his knees to bend as he climbed. He had to bring his feet out and round with an awkward, splay-footed movement. The temptation to look down to see that his foot was firmly on the next rung was strong, but he remembered the warning and kept his head rigidly level.

But if it would have been frightening to look down, it was nearly as frightening to look straight ahead. Always before when he had climbed a ladder, the wall had been comfortingly close. This time it was far away.[1] He was alone in space. He had not reckoned with the ladder being so far from the wall. It brought a sudden qualm of helplessness and sickness, and in desperation he threw his head back and looked upwards. The rungs of the ladder rushed away from him in frightening perspective. But looking upwards he could forget his awkwardly-groping feet, and at the top, just to the left, he could see the foreshortened black square of Lucian's back, which steadied him slightly.

NIGEL BALCHIN:

Mine Own Executioner (Collins, 1945)

[1] Add a phrase to make the meaning clear in French—*e.g.* "in front of him."

7

*A BURNING CARGO***

The captain gave his orders, and once more the *Pyrenees* swung off for another run across the inhospitable sea.

And the middle of the next[1] afternoon saw[2] despair and mutiny[3] on her smoking deck. The current had accelerated, the wind had slackened, and the *Pyrenees* had sagged off to the west. The look-out sighted Barclay de Tolley to the eastward, barely visible from the masthead, and vainly and for hours the *Pyrenees* tried to beat up to it. Ever, like a mirage, the coconut trees hovered on the horizon, visible only from the masthead. From the deck they were hidden by the bulge of the world.

Again Captain Davenport consulted McCoy and the chart. Makemo lay seventy-five miles to the south-west. Its lagoon was thirty miles long, and its entrance was excellent. When Captain Davenport gave his orders, the crew refused duty. They announced that they had had enough of hell-fire under their feet. There was the land. What if the ship could not make it? They could make it in the boats. Let her burn, then. Their lives[4] amounted to something to them. They had served faithfully the ship, now they were going to serve themselves.

They sprang to the boats, brushing the second and third mates out of the way, and proceeded to swing the boats out and to prepare to lower away. Captain Davenport and the first mate, revolvers[5] in hand, were advancing to the break of the poop, when McCoy, who had climbed on top of the cabin, began to speak.

JACK LONDON:

"The Seed of McCoy" from *South Sea Tales* (Macmillan N.Y., 1911)

[1] Translate: "the next day, about the middle," etc.

[2] Translate: "one saw."

[3] "despair and mutiny": use a word—*e.g.*, "crew"—to connect and explain the two words.

[4] § **178**. 1.

[5] § **178**. 2.

8

*AN ESTRANGEMENT****

Hardly a week passed now without some bitter quarrel. I seemed to be perpetually stealing out of sound of angry voices; fearful of being made the butt of my father's serene taunts, of my mother's passions and desperate remorse. He disdained to defend himself against her, never reasoned with her; he merely shrugged his shoulders, denied her charges, ignored her anger; coldly endeavouring only to show his indifference, to conceal by every means in his power his own inward weariness and vexation. I saw this, of course, only vaguely, yet with all a child's certainty of insight, though I rarely knew the cause of my misery; and I continued to love them both in my selfish fashion, not a whit the less.

At last, on St Valentine's Day, things came to a worse pass than ever. It had always been my father's custom to hang my mother a valentine on the handle of her little parlour door, a string of pearls, a fan, a book of poetry, whatever it might be. She came down early this morning, and sat in the window-seat, looking out at the falling snow. She said nothing at breakfast, only feigned to eat, lifting her eyes at intervals to glance at my father with a strange intensity, as if of hatred, tapping her foot on the floor. He took no notice of her, sat quiet and moody with his own thoughts. I think he had not really forgotten the day, for I found long afterwards in his old bureau a bracelet purchased but a week before with her name written on a scrap of paper, inside the case. Yet it seemed to be the absence of this little gift that had driven my mother beyond reason.

Towards evening, tired of the house, tired of being alone, I went out and played for a while listlessly in the snow. At nightfall I went in. My father came out of the dining-room and looked at me in silence, standing in the gloom of the wintry dusk. My mother followed him. I can see her now, leaning in the doorway.

WALTER DE LA MARE:
"The Almond Tree" from *Best Short Stories of Walter de la Mare* (Faber and Faber, 1945)

9

*WAITING FOR A CHANNEL BOAT****

When he reached the landing-stage at the head of the pier he found quite a number of persons awaiting the arrival of the boat from the Continent. These persons had already assumed that unique look which is always faintly uncomfortable to any newcomer; the peculiar look of human beings whose protracted waiting has given them a malicious uniformity. Any casual[1] group of people who meet in common subjection to the waywardness of chance come to assume certain characteristics which humanity displays at no other time. At first they are totally unaware of one another, even more indifferent than if they passed on the street. But very quickly they become definitely *inter-conscious* and at first this takes the form of a vague, almost indecent awareness of one another. It is *after* this, when they have begun to get used to wondering critically about one another, that it is so especially awkward to be the last newcomer who joins their malignant vigil.

This was the precise role that Magnus was now destined to fill; and he very quickly found the situation so intolerable that, having ascertained from a luggage-porter that the boat's delay at the harbour's entrance had something to do with the tide and would probably be protracted for some while yet, he paid his sixpence and entered the enclosed portion of the pleasure-pier, from the end of which he knew that he would be almost able to shout to anyone on[2] the steamer's deck.

JOHN COWPER POWYS:
Jobber Skald (John Lane, 1935)

[1] "casual": use an adverb after "meet."
[2] "on": insert an explanatory phrase.

10

*AN UNEASY VIGIL*****

One evening—with nothing to lead up or prepare it—I felt the cold touch of the impression that had breathed on me the night of my arrival and which, much lighter then as I have mentioned, I should probably have made little of in memory had my subsequent sojourn been less agitated. I had not gone to bed; I sat reading by a couple of candles. There was a roomful of old books at Bly—last-century fiction some of it, which, to the extent of a distinctly deprecated renown, but never to so much as that of a stray specimen, had reached the sequestered home and appealed to the unavowed curiosity of my youth. I remember that the book I had in my hand was Fielding's *Amelia*; also that I was wholly awake. I recall further both a general conviction that it was horribly late and a particular objection to looking at my watch. I figured finally that the white curtain draping, in the fashion of those days, the head of Flora's little bed, shrouded, as I had assured myself long before, the perfection of childish rest. I recollect in short that though I was deeply interested in my author I found myself, at the turn of a page and with his spell all scattered, looking straight up from him and hard at the door of my room. There was a moment during which I listened, reminded of the faint sense I had had, the first night, of there being something undefinably astir in the house, and noted the soft breath of the open casement just move the half-drawn blind. Then, with all the marks of a deliberation that must have seemed magnificent had there been any one to admire it, I laid down my book, rose to my feet and, taking a candle, went straight out of the room and, from the passage, on which my light made little impression, noiselessly closed and locked the door.

HENRY JAMES:
The Turn of the Screw (Heinemann, 1898)

II

*A BOUT OF SEASICKNESS***

In his sleeping cabin he fell across his cot, and lay[1] there for twenty minutes before he could rouse himself to sit up. Then he dragged off his two coats,[2] and, still wearing his shirt and waistcoat and breeches, he got under the blankets with a groan. The ship was pitching remorselessly as[3] she ran before the wind, and all the timbers complained in spasmodic chorus. Hornblower set his teeth at every heave, while the cot in which he lay soared upward twenty feet or more and then sank hideously downward under the influence of each successive wave. Nevertheless, with no possibility of consecutive thinking, it was easy for exhaustion to step in. He was so tired that with his mind empty he fell asleep in a few minutes, motion and noise and seasickness notwithstanding.

So deeply did he sleep that when he awoke he had to think for a moment before he realised where he was. The heaving and tossing, of which he first became conscious, was familiar and yet unexpected. The door into the after cabin, hooked open, admitted a tiny amount of grey light, in which he blinked round him. Then, simultaneously with the return of recollection, his stomach heaved again. He got precariously to his feet, staggered across the after cabin, to the rail of the stern gallery, and then peered miserably across the grey sea in the first faint light of dawn, with the wind whipping round him. There was no sail in sight from there, and the consequent apprehension helped him to recover himself. Putting on coat and greatcoat again, he walked up to the quarterdeck.

C. S. Forester:

A Ship of the Line (Michael Joseph, 1938)

[1] Does this verb evoke state or action? See § **116.** 2. (*c*).
[2] French has no general term equivalent to "coats." Specify.
[3] *Comme*? *En*+gerund? *A mesure que*?

12

*A MINING DISASTER****

During the school dinner there was news. The radio smoothly spoke of 'disaster,' of 'feared loss of life,' of rescue attempts, of pithead crowds. A few mothers came for their children, careful to see that they had their dinner before leaving. There were also white-faced relatives who came, surprising children and leading them silently away to bereaved homes. Miss Trotter was too busy to talk much, but it was soon common knowledge that the explosion had killed some outright; that others were missing, sealed off by the fall in the pit; that there had been a trickle of survivors, Tommy Roxford, the promising boxer, among them.

The traffic was coming down Tanglewood Lane by the end of the school dinner, ambulances moving cautiously, jangling their bells. The children watched them from the playground wall. When Miss Trotter had cleaned up the dinner, she went out along the wall, saying little, but in her strange, magnetic way comforting the children. When it was nearly time for afternoon school, she took off her glasses and stared across the main road towards the winding gear of Tanglewood on the skyline.

Mr Hawes rang the bell and said: "School as usual this afternoon, please, Miss Trotter. I dare say there may be a few people coming up here to take children away—you know why. But we try not to let such things interfere with routine. Children are creatures of habit after all, and we are here to serve the children." He said this almost as if he was excusing himself, speaking in the concise, pedantic voice he used for school inspectors, patting the shoulders of the children as they passed him to go into the classrooms with that gesture of his which was familiar to generation after generation of Birely folk.

JOHN PUDNEY:

"The Explosion" from *World Prize Stories* (Odhams, 1952)

13

*SLEEPING ROUGH***

It[1] was cold on the bench. For the first hour or two he was grateful that, at least, it wasn't raining, but after about one o'clock the cold became so intense that it could certainly not have been worse even if he had been soaking wet. There must be some knack of sleeping on these things; one more lesson that he had still to learn. You mustn't lie down, he knew that, or a policeman could pull you in. You must keep sitting up and looking more or less as if you were awake. He tried drawing his knees up and hunching his body into a tight ball, then clasping his hands round his knees, leaning his head forward, and relaxing as far as possible with his fingers interlaced. But somehow it seemed to cramp the muscles of his back, and after about ten minutes he abandoned it. That was about every position he could think of: all no good. The clear chimes of some City clock came through the cold air. One-fifteen. A night or two without sleep didn't necessarily harm you, if you were fit. Walk about a bit. He dragged himself along by the side of the quietly lapping, malevolent river. A litter box of wire-netting attracted his attention by gleaming whitely: it was full of sheets of newspaper. A piece of luck. One of the easiest ways of keeping warm. He stuffed loosely-rolled pads of it into the bottoms of his trousers, up to the knees, and inside his jacket. One or two sheets were rather greasy, as if they had been used for wrapping fish and chips.

JOHN WAIN:

Hurry on Down (Secker and Warburg, 1953)

[1] Use *on*. Add a term denoting attitude or position.

14

*HIGH SPEED ON A MOTOR CYCLE*****

Boa is a top-gear machine, as sweet in that as most single-cylinders in middle. I chugged lordlily past the guardroom and through the speed limit at no more than sixteen. Round the bend, past the farm, and the way straightens. Now for it. The engine's final development is 52 horse-power. A miracle that all this docile strength waits behind one tiny lever for the pleasure of my hand.

Another bend, and I have the honour of one of England's straightest and fastest roads. The burble of my exhaust unwound like a cord behind me. Soon my speed snapped it, and I heard only the cry of the wind which my battering head split and fended aside. The cry rose with my speed to a shriek: while the air's coldness streamed like two jets of iced water into my dissolving eyes. I screwed them to slits and focused my sight two hundred yards ahead of me on the empty mosaic of the tar's gravelled undulations.

Like arrows the tiny flies pricked my cheeks; and sometimes a heavier body, some house-fly or beetle, would crash into face or lips like a spent bullet. A glance at the speedometer: 78. Boanerges was warming up. I pulled the throttle right open on the top of the slope, and we swooped flying across the dip and up-down, up-down the switchback beyond: the weighty machine launching itself like a projectile with a whirr of wheels into the air at the take-off of each rise, to land lurchingly with such a snatch of the driving chain as jerked my spine like a rictus.

T. E. Lawrence:
The Mint (Jonathan Cape, 1955)

15

*A TEST MATCH****

After ten minutes another bumper glanced off Compton's right elbow into slips—fifth ball of Lindwall's eighth over. As the fast bowler delivered the next ball his feet travelled too far for Umpire Dai Davies, who called "No ball!" The ball pitched short but did not fly so high. Compton was moving in front to glide it to leg when he heard the umpire's shout, tried to change the stroke to a hook and edged the rising ball to his forehead. As the ball cannoned 40 yards through the air to fine-leg the stunned batsman staggered. Miller ran from the slips to support him. Bradman and Johnson helped him off, sagging at the knees, with Miller holding a handkerchief to staunch the flow of blood from an inch-long gash between his eyes. Two stitches closed it.

Compton is as hardy as he is handsome. Little more than an hour later he ate lunch. After a trial at the nets against Pollard, Wardle and Young, the fall of Edrich brought his reappearance less than 3½ hours after he had been assisted into the pavilion. Lindwall met England's hero, and the pair exchanged smiling remarks. Looking around a diagonal inch of plaster between his brows, Compton could see that the board showed half England's wickets gone for[1] only 119, and that the bowler he would have to face was . . . Lindwall. Nerve triumphed. His batting raised the crowd from the dumps. Not one gingerly shot. He played fully forward or wholly back, bowing over those delicate leg-glides which he makes with feet together and scarcely more than a bat's thickness between the ball and his knees. His lightness of touch gave no sign that he was again supporting the weight of England's sagging innings like an oak beam. Two more wickets fell that afternoon but, aided by the fortune that ought to favour the brave, Compton was 64 not out at the end of the day, in which Lindwall bounced seven balls in 26 overs. Two more of them rose rib-high to Compton, who stopped them with a dead bat; after the last one he played a theoretical hook, in retrospect. In London's *Daily Herald*, Charles Bray's report carried the headline: *Compton Saves England's Face at the Expense of His Own.*

RAY ROBINSON:

From the Boundary (Collins, 1951)

[1] Expand: *e.g.*, "the number of runs was only" etc.

16

*A MORAL TALE**

Once upon a time three poor students, all very near-sighted, and each possessing a single pair of horn-rimmed spectacles, set out to walk to a remote university, for the purpose of competing for a professorship.

On the way, while sleeping by the road-side, a thief stole their three pairs of horn-rimmed spectacles.

Waking, their distress was great: they stumbled, they fell, they lost their way; and night was at hand, when they met a pedlar.

"Have you any spectacles?" said the three miserable students.

"Yes," said the pedlar, "exactly three pairs; but they are set in gold, and with magnificent workmanship; in fact, they were made for the king, and they cost so much——"

"Such a sum," said the students, "is absurd; it is nearly as much as we possess."

"I cannot," the pedlar replied, "take less; but here is an ivory-handled[1] frying-pan which I can let you have for a trifling sum, and I strongly recommend you to buy it because it is such an astonishing bargain, and you may never again chance to meet with a similarly joyful opportunity."

Said the eldest of the three students, "I will grope my way on as I can. It is ridiculous to buy a pair of this man's[2] spectacles at such a price."

"And I," said the second, "am determined to purchase the

ivory-handled frying-pan; it costs little, and will be very useful, and I may never again have such an extraordinary bargain."

But the youngest of the three, undisturbed by the laughter of the two others, bought the gold-rimmed sumptuous spectacles, and was soon out of sight.

Thereon, No. 1 set off slowly, but, falling into a ditch by reason of his blindness, broke his leg, and was carried back, by a charitable passer-by in a cart,[3] to his native town.

No. 2 wandered on, but lost his way inextricably, and, after much suffering, was obliged to sell his ivory-handled frying-pan at a great loss, to enable him to return home.

No. 3 reached the University, gained the prize, and was made Professor of Grumphiology, with a house and fixed salary, and lived happily ever after.

Moral.—To pay much for what is most useful, is wiser than to pay little for what is not so.[4]

EDWARD LEAR:

The Journal of a Landscape Painter in Corsica

[1] § **282**. 3. (*c*).

[2] Translate: "a pair of spectacles from this man."

[3] Arrange the adverbial phrases to avoid the ambiguity of the English.

[4] § **223**. 1.

17

*SINISTER INTENTIONS**

They boarded the bus and were carried swiftly towards Sheraton Road where Kelpey lived. Neither[1] of them spoke. They sat inside the vehicle, with[2] their hats on their knees. At this time of the evening, there were few passengers, and the conductor had time to study Smith and Lane as they sat side by side, erect, not talking, their eyes looking straight ahead. They had an unmistakable suggestion of the foreign, the unfamiliar, about them. The indescribable mode of behaviour and the slight difference of cut and texture of their clothes made it obvious. Who were they? What was their errand?

A little later, they alighted. As[3] they passed the conductor, he had a better opportunity in which to study them. He noticed that they had an expression of sullen concentration. He signalled the bus to proceed, then he leaned out and watched them. They went towards Sheraton Road, in step, erect, like men marching. Then, almost as though by design, they broke step, opened their jackets and lounged slowly along. It was like an act of deception, to allay suspicion. But their progress was heavy with purpose. Too heavy! Where . . . in what particular place . . . had he seen them before? He remembered them. He would continue to remember them.

Smith and Lane entered Sheraton Road and walked towards Kelpey's home. They knew the house. They were only a few yards from[4] it when Smith put a hand on Lane's arm and tried to stop him.

F. L. Green:

On the Edge of the Sea (Michael Joseph, 1944)

[1] § **436.** [2] § **178.** 2.
[3] *Comme? Lorsque? A mesure que?* [4] § **282.** 1. (*b*).

18

*A FAIRGROUND SCENE*****

Aimlessly drifting, dazed in the kaleidoscopic confusion of sensory impressions, flares of lights assailed her, shouts of showmen; moving bodies jostled her, bodies that would not move, lumpishly fixed, staring before some stall; crash of china smote her, ceaseless knocking, wooden, hollow, ceaseless thump and bump of balls, ninepins, coconuts; smell of trampled grass, of beer, cigarette ends, pervasive smell of people, whistle and shriek of sirens, shiver of tambourines, metallic, brassy blare of merry-go-rounds, mournfully trumpeting, hot-sounding. Above her the swing-boats creaked, shook, shot up, shot down, so fast, so giddily, she could not look. Over the top they'd go, surely, surely. They'd be tipped out. The danger of it! And the switchbacks, whizzing downhill on their shaky wooden scaffolding, with that horrible roar! Listen to the people yelling! And those little motor cars bumping into each other—didn't the people look silly sitting behind the toy steering-wheels! . . .

That music, how loud it was, it fairly hurt one's ears! Round and round the couples rode, as quiet as quiet, smiling a bit, dreamy-looking; and one little boy, been there all the evening, pennyworth after pennyworth, now on an ostrich, now on a horse. He'd be sick, he would, sooner or later. The whirl slackened, the tune stopped, lights ceased from spinning. E. Pettigrew's Grand Electric Leaping Animals, she read: all sorts of funny birds and beasts. They went on turning, turning, after the music, slower and slower, in a kind of sick way. That kid was off at last, feeling in his grubby pockets. Empty. No more rides.

ROSAMUND LEHMANN:
A Note in Music (Chatto and Windus, 1930)

19

*MOUNTING TENSION****

It was the week before Christmas, and George Links could not help but be aware that the thunderous surf of the festive season was beating against the household and being stormily repulsed, as by a lighthouse. Christmas cards dropped through the letter-box at intervals increasingly short and decreasingly predictable. Janet always gathered them up from the mat, and always, after a perfunctory glance at the signatures, put them in a neat pile on top of the bookcase in the living-room. The pile grew and grew, and tragic discontent radiated from it. Janet's refusal to stand the cards up where they could be seen, the flat and uncompromising way she laid them tidily on top of one another, expressed more clearly than words that she had given up caring. She had completely withdrawn her emotions from the home they had built up: George Links understood this, and, with a dry pang that went too deep to be felt as ordinary suffering, he accepted it. The Christmas cards lay on their sides, one above the other, like kind words locked away where they could never be heard.

Nevertheless, the only times, during that week, when George Links felt that his calm was in danger were the moments when he was racked by the wild impulse to hurry off at once to London, irrupt into the Cowley household, and plunge the drama there and then into its last scene. But these fits never lasted long. Deeply, he knew that this period of waiting, of forcing himself to let the pre-arranged time come round, was a necessary preliminary discipline. The task was not, in any case, going to be easy; by rushing into it in a dishevelled way, giving the impression that he was acting from nerve-sick impulsiveness rather than cast-iron, manly resolve, he would only make it ten times harder.

JOHN WAIN:
A Travelling Woman (Macmillan, 1959)

20

*A NERVOUS TRAVELLER IN FRANCE****

Before they had got any distance, it became clear to Mary that Richard's travelling-days were . . . well, one could hardly say "over," when they had only just begun. The truth was, they had come too late. He was no longer able to enjoy them.

It was not the physical discomforts alone that defeated him. The fancies he went in for, as soon as he set foot on foreign soil, made his life a misery to him. In Paris, for instance, he was seized by a nervous fear of the street traffic; actually felt afraid he was going to be run over. If he had to cross one of the vast squares, over which vehicles dashed from all directions, he would stand and hesitate on the kerb, looking from side to side, unable to resolve to take the plunge; and wasn't he angry with her, if she tried to make a dash for it! His own fears rendered him fussy about Cuffy and the maid's safety, too. He wouldn't hear of them going out alone; and insisted every morning on shepherding them to their walk in the Public Gardens. If he was prevented, they must drive there in a *fiacre*. Which all helped to make the stay in Paris both troublesome and costly. Then there was that time in Strasbourg when they set out to climb the tower of the cathedral. It was certainly a bad day to choose, for it had rained in the night and afterwards frozen over, and even the streets were slippery. But Richard was bent on seeing the Rhine, and the Vosges, and the Black Forest from the top of the steeple; so up they went. As far as the platform, it was plain sailing. But on the tower proper, when they were mounting the innumerable stone steps—all glassy with ice, and very tricky to keep a footing on—which led to the spire, he turned pale, and confessed to giddiness.

H. H. RICHARDSON:

The Fortunes of Richard Mahoney (Heinemann, 1930)

21

*CAUGHT AT THE CUSTOMS**

"Please open the blue bag."

I had two bags. A blue one and a brown one. The blue one contained all the things I had bought in London, the brown one contained dirty laundry and old suits.

I started to open the brown one.

The customs officer shook his head. "The blue one."

I slowly opened the blue one. His eyes popped open and a gleeful expression appeared on his face. "New clothes. You didn't declare them."

"Are you supposed to declare new clothes?"

"Take his passport away," the customs officer said to another one who apparently was under his command, "and bring the bags to the customs office."

The second man saluted me, smiled in an embarrassed way, called a porter to take the bags and I was escorted by two uniformed men to the customs office. It was apparent to everyone in the station that I had been caught, and there were smiles on every face as I walked what could very well have been my last mile.

At the office my guards saluted me again. The man who had caught me was waiting for me and said to his assistants: "Take out everything."

By the time[1] they had finished, the entire office was covered with contraband. Several other officers came in to stare at the haul. They shook hands with the officer who had caught me, and congratulated him. I was caught up in the excitement, and I congratulated him also. I even offered him a cigar.

He said he didn't smoke; he had given it up about a year ago.

I congratulated him on this also.

Then he started listing all the items and their value. I had cleverly left on the price tags. On the few things that had no price tags, we argued back and forth and occasionally called in a neutral customs officer to arbitrate.

Finally, when everything was listed, I helped add up the figures for him, and in two hours we had arrived at a sum. With the fine which he said I'd have to pay, it came to 50,000 francs (about $140). I had to call[2] my wife to bring me the money.

ART BUCHWALD:
More Caviar (Gollancz, 1958)

[1] *Quand*. See § **395**. 2. *Note* 1. [2] *i.e.*, "telephone."

22

*LUNCHING OUT IN A TIME OF RATIONING****

At two minutes before half past twelve every day, Plymbell was first in the queue in the foyer outside the locked glass doors of Polli's Restaurant, a few yards from his shop. On one side of the glass Plymbell floated—handsome, Roman, silver-haired, as white-skinned and consequent as a turbot of fifty; on the other side of the glass, in the next aquarium, stood Polli with the key in his hand waiting for the clock to strike the half-hour—a man liverish and suspended in misanthropy like a tench in the weed of a canal. Plymbell stared clean through Polli to the sixty empty tables beyond; Polli stared clean through the middle of Plymbell into the miasma of the restaurant keeper's life. Two fish gazed with the indifference of creatures who had accepted the fact that neither of them was edible. What they wanted, what the whole of England was crying for, was not fish but red meat, and to get meat at Polli's one had to be there at half past twelve, on the dot.

First customer in was Plymbell. He had his table, in the middle of this chipped Edwardian place, with his back to one of those white pillars that gave it the appearance of a shop-soiled wedding cake mounted on a red carpet, and he faced the serving-hatch. Putting up a monocle to his more annoyed eye, he watched the chef standing over his pans, and while he watched he tapped the table with lightly frantic fingers. Polli's waiters were old men, and the one who served Plymbell had the dejected smirk of a convict.

V. S. PRITCHETT:
"The Satisfactory" from *Winter's Tales I*
(Macmillan, 1955)

23

*A MUSICAL PARTY***

Afterwards there was an interval, during which everybody ate and drank and smoked and talked all at once, and a girl who appeared to be a secretary at some legation came up with Something-insky and another, older man, and the girl who was a secretary was very giddy and gay and apparently rather tight, though not unpleasantly so,[1] and then a little foreign girl with a hideous fur-trimmed jacket joined them, and the six of them made a little group in one corner, where they ate and drank and smoked and talked as hard as anybody. Then the little hostess screamed again, and this time the tall host produced a number of astonishing syllables in a rasping tenor and then put on a colossal smile, and at once everybody sat down somewhere and most of the lights were turned out. Only the corner where the Jew still sat at the piano was fully illuminated. Then there appeared in front of the piano a smallish plump man with an enormous bald head and yellow fat face, who stood there, smiling vaguely at them while they applauded, like another but alien[2] Humpty-Dumpty. The Jew played a few sonorous and melancholy chords. Humpty-Dumpty put his hand to his mouth, as if to press a button, for when he lowered his hand his face was quite different; the smile had been wiped off; his eye-brows had descended at least an inch and a half; and his eyes stared tragically out of deep hollows. Miss Matfield noticed all these details.

J. B. PRIESTLEY:
Angel Pavement (Heinemann, 1930)

[1] Clarify by expanding the phrase.
[2] "but alien." Translate after the noun and expand as necessary.

24

*A FIGHTER PILOT BALES OUT*****

He tore his helmet and mask off and yanked the little rubber ball over his head—the hood ripped away and screaming noise battered at him. Out came the harness pin and he gripped the cockpit rim to lever himself up, wondering if he could get out without thrust from the helpless legs. He struggled madly to get his head above the windscreen, and suddenly felt he was being sucked out as the tearing wind caught him.

Top half out. He was out! No, something had him by the leg holding him. (The rigid foot of the right leg hooked fast in some vice in the cockpit.) Then the nightmare took his exposed body and beat him and screamed and roared in his ears as the broken fighter dragging him by the leg plunged down and spun and battered him and the wind clawed at his flesh and the cringing sightless eyeballs. It went on and on into confusion, on and on, timeless, witless and helpless, with a little core of thought deep under the blind head fighting for life in the wilderness. It said he had a hand gripping the D-ring of the parachute and mustn't take it off, must grip it because the wind wouldn't let him get it back again, and he mustn't pull it or the wind would split his parachute because they must be going 500 miles an hour. On and on . . . till the steel and leather snapped.

He was floating, in peace. The noise and buffeting had stopped. Floating upwards? He thought it is so quiet I must have a rest. I would like to go to sleep.

In a flash the brain cleared and he knew and pulled the D-ring, hearing a crack as the parachute opened. Then he was actually floating. High above the sky was still blue, and right at his feet lay a veil of cloud. He sank into it. That was the cloud at 4,000 feet. Cutting it fine! In seconds he dropped easily under it and saw the earth, green and dappled, where the sun struck through. Something flapped in his face and he saw it was his right trouser leg, split along the seam.

PAUL BRICKHILL:
Reach for the Sky (Collins, 1954)

25

*PENDENNIS IN LOVE***

We are not going to say a great deal about Pen's courtship of Miss Fotheringay, for the reader has already had a specimen of her conversation, much of which need surely not be reported. Pen sat with her hour after hour, and poured forth all his honest boyish soul to her. Everything he knew, or hoped, or felt, or had read, or fancied, he told to her.[1] He never tired of talking and longing. One after another, as his thoughts rose in his hot eager brain, he clothed them in words, and told them to her. Her part of the *tête à tête* was not to talk, but to appear as if she understood what Pen talked, and to look exceedingly handsome and sympathising. The fact is, whilst he was making one of his tirades, the lovely Emily, who could not comprehend a tenth part of his talk, had leisure to think about her own affairs, and would arrange in her own mind how they should dress the cold mutton, or how she would turn the black satin, or make herself out of her scarf a bonnet like Miss Thackthwaite's new one,[2] and so forth. Pen spouted Byron and Moore; passion and poetry: her business was to throw up her eyes, or fixing them for a moment on his face, to cry, "Oh, 'tis beautiful! Ah, how exquisite! Repeat those lines again." And off the boy went,[3] and she returned to her own simple thoughts about the turned gown, or the hashed mutton.

In fact Pen's passion was not long a secret from the lovely Emily or her father. Upon his second visit, his admiration was quite evident to both of them, and on his departure the old gentleman said to his daughter, as he winked at her over his glass of grog, "Faith, Milly darling, I think ye've hooked that chap."

W. M. THACKERAY:
Pendennis

[1] § **223**.
[2] Translate: "the one Miss Thackthwaite had just bought."
[3] The historical infinitive might be used here. See § **109**.

26

*A MYSTERIOUS PRESENCE**

Tom's adventure happened during the second week of his stay. All the people about the place had gone to sleep for the night but, as he[1] could not sleep, he arose silently and came down out of the hay-loft carrying his blanket. It was a silent, hot, soft night without a moon and he went to where there was a small grass plot that came down to the barn, and spreading his blanket sat with his back to the wall of the barn.

That he could not sleep did not matter. He was young and strong. "If I do not sleep to-night I will sleep to-morrow night," he thought. There was something in the air that he thought concerned only himself, and that made him want to be thus awake, sitting out of doors and looking at the dim distant trees in the apple orchard near the barn, at the stars in the sky, at the farm-house, faintly seen some few hundred feet away.[2] Now that he was out of doors he no longer felt restless. Perhaps[3] it was only that he was nearer something that was like himself at the moment, just the night perhaps.

He became aware of something, of something moving restlessly in the darkness. There was a fence between the farm-yard and the orchard, with[4] berry bushes growing[4] beside it, and something was moving in the darkness along the berry bushes. Was[5] it a cow that had got out of the stable or were the bushes moved by a wind?

SHERWOOD ANDERSON:
"A Chicago Hamlet" from *Horses and Men* (Jonathan Cape, 1924)

[1] Stress. See § **234**. 2.
[2] § **282**. 1. (*b*).
[3] § **344**. 1.
[4] Use a relative clause.
[5] § **83**. 3. § **84**. 1.

27

*LORD PETER ON THE MOORS***

Behind Riddlesdale Lodge the moor stretched starkly away and upward. The heather was brown and wet, and the little streams had no colour in them. It was six o'clock, but there was no sunset. Only a paleness had moved behind the thick sky from east to west all day. Lord Peter, tramping back[1] after a long and fruitless search for tidings of the man with the motor-cycle, voiced the dull suffering of his gregarious spirit. "I wish old Parker was here," he muttered, and squelched down a sheep-track.

He was making, not directly for the Lodge, but for a farm-house about two and a half miles distant from it, known as Grider's Hole. It lay almost due north of Riddlesdale village, a[2] lonely outpost on the edge of the moor, in a valley of fertile land between two wide swells of heather. The track wound down from the height called Whemmeling Fell, skirted a vile swamp, and crossed the little River Ridd about half a mile before reaching the farm. Peter had small hope of hearing any news at Grider's Hole, but he was filled with a sullen determination to leave no stone unturned. Privately, however, he felt convinced that the motor-cycle had come by the high road, Parker's investigations notwithstanding, and perhaps passed directly through King's Fenton without stopping or[3] attracting attention. Still, he had said he would search the neighbourhood, and Grider's Hole was in the neighbourhood. He paused to relight his pipe, then squelched steadily on. The path was marked with stout white posts at regular intervals, and presently with hurdles. The reason for this was apparent as one came to the bottom of the valley, for only a few yards on the left began the stretch of rough, reedy tussocks, with slobbering black bog between them, in which anything heavier than a water-wagtail would speedily suffer change into a succession of little bubbles.

DOROTHY L. SAYERS:
Clouds of Witness (Allen and Unwin, 1927)

[1] Translate: "on the road back." [2] § **170**. 4. [3] *et.*

28

*A PRIZE FIGHT*****

In the first round every one thought it was all over. After making play a short time, the Gasman flew at his adversary like a tiger, struck five blows in as many seconds, three first, and then following him as he staggered back, two more, right and left, and down he fell, a mighty ruin. There was a shout, and I said, "There is no standing this." Neate seemed like a lifeless lump of flesh and bone, round which the Gasman's blows played with the rapidity of electricity or lightning, and you imagined he would only be lifted up to be knocked down again. It was as if Hickman held a sword or a fire in that right hand of his, and directed it against an unarmed body. They met again, and Neate seemed, not cowed, but particularly cautious. I saw his teeth clenched together and his brows knit close against the sun. He held out both his arms at full length straight before him, like two sledge hammers, and raised his left an inch or two higher. The Gasman could not get over this guard—they struck mutually and fell, but without advantage on either side. It was the same in the next round; but the balance of power was thus restored—the fate of the battle was suspended. No one could tell how it would end. This was the only moment in which opinion was divided; for, in the next, the Gasman aiming a mortal blow at his adversary's neck, with his right hand, and failing from the length he had to reach, the other returned it with his left at full swing, planted a tremendous blow on his cheek-bone and eyebrow, and made a red ruin of that side of his face. The Gasman went down, and there was another shout—a roar of triumph as the waves of fortune rolled tumultuously from side to side. This was a settler. Hickman got up, and 'grinned horrible a ghastly smile,' yet he was evidently dashed in his opinion of himself; it was the first time he had ever been so punished; all one side of his face was perfect scarlet, and his right eye was closed in dingy blackness, as he advanced to the fight, less confident, but still determined.

WILLIAM HAZLITT:
"The Fight" from *Essays*

29

*A WOOD BEWITCHED****

Again the sun flamed out abruptly and lit the floor of the wood with pools of silver, and at the same moment a violent gust of wind passed shouting overhead. Drops fell clattering everywhere upon the leaves, making a sharp pattering as of many footsteps. The whole copse shuddered and went moving.

"Rain, by George!" thought the clerk, and, feeling for his umbrella, discovered he had lost it. He turned back to the gate and found it lying on the farther side. To his amazement he saw the fields at the far end of the glade, the red house, too, ashine in the sunset. He laughed then, for, of course, in his struggle with the gate, he had somehow got turned round—had fallen back instead of forwards. Climbing over, this time quite easily, he retraced his steps. The silver band, he saw, had been torn from the umbrella.

No doubt his foot, a nail, or something, had caught in it and ripped it off. The clerk began to run; he felt extraordinarily dismayed.

But, while he ran, the entire wood ran with him, round him, to and fro, trees shifting like living things, leaves folding and unfolding, trunks darting backwards and forwards, and branches disclosing enormous empty spaces, then closing up again before he could look into them. There were footsteps everywhere, and laughing, crying voices, and crowds of figures gathering just behind his back till the glade, he knew, was thick with moving life.

The wind in his ears, of course, produced the voices and the laughter, while sun and clouds, plunging the copse alternately in shadow and bright dazzling light, created the figures. But he did not like it, and he went as fast as ever his sturdy legs could take him. He was frightened now. This was no story for his wife and children. He ran like the wind. But his feet made no sound upon the soft mossy turf.

Then, to his horror, he saw that the glade grew narrow, nettles and weeds stood thick across it, it dwindled down into a tiny path, and twenty yards ahead it stopped finally and melted off among the trees.

ALGERNON BLACKWOOD:
"Ancient Lights" from *Ten Minute Stories* (Murray, 1914)

30

*ESCAPE FROM A MOB***

The fact emerges that about three o'clock on Sunday afternoon a remarkably big and ugly London crowd, entirely out of hand, came rolling down Thursday Street intent on Bensington's exemplary death as a warning to all scientific investigators, and that it came[1] nearer accomplishing its object than any London crowd has ever come[2] since[3] the Hyde Park railings came down in remote middle Victorian times. This crowd came so close to its object indeed, that for the space of an hour or more a word would have settled the unfortunate gentleman's fate.

The first intimation he had of the thing was the noise of the people outside. He went to the window and peered, realising nothing of what impended. For a minute perhaps he watched them seething about the entrance, disposing of an ineffectual dozen of policemen who barred their way, before he fully realised his own importance in the affair. It came upon him in a flash—that that roaring, swaying multitude was after him.[4] He was all alone in the flat—fortunately perhaps—his cousin Jane having gone down to Ealing to have tea with a relation on her mother's side, and he had no more idea of how to behave under such circumstances than he had of the etiquette of the Day of Judgment. He was still dashing about the flat asking his furniture what he should do, turning keys in locks and then unlocking them again, making darts at door and window and bedroom—when the floor clerk came to him.

"There isn't a moment, Sir," he said. "They've got your number from the board in the hall! They're coming straight up!"

He ran Mr Bensington out into the passage, already echoing with the approaching tumult from the great staircase, locked the door behind them, and led the way into the opposite flat by means of his duplicate key.

H. G. WELLS:
The Food of the Gods (Newnes, 1915)

[1] Use *être*. Tense? [2] § **223**.

[3] Translate: "since that far-off day in middle Victorian times when" etc. [4] Stress "him." § **324**. 4.

31

*A LETTER FROM WONDERLAND**

It's been so frightfully hot here that I've been too weak to hold a pen, and even if I had been able,[1] there was no ink—it had all[2] evaporated into a cloud of black steam, and in that state it has been floating about the room, inking the walls and ceiling till they're hardly fit to be seen: to-day it is cooler, and a little has come back into the ink-bottle in the form of black snow.

This hot weather makes me very sad and sulky: I can hardly keep my temper sometimes. For instance, just now the Bishop of Oxford came to see me—it was a civil thing to do, and he meant no harm, poor man: but I was so provoked at his coming in that I threw a book at his head, which I am afraid hurt him a good deal.

This isn't quite true—so you needn't believe it. Don't be in such a hurry to believe next time—I'll tell you why: If you set to work to believe everything, you will tire out the muscles of your mind, and then you'll be so weak you won't be able to believe the simplest true things. Only last week a friend of mine set to work to believe Jack-the-giant-killer. He managed to do it, but he was so exhausted by it that when I told him it was raining (which was true) he *couldn't* believe it, but rushed out into the street without his hat or umbrella, the consequence of which was his hair got seriously damp, and one curl didn't recover its right shape for nearly two days.

LEWIS CARROLL:
Letters from Wonderland

[1] § **223**. [2] Adjective, pronoun or adverb? See § **247**., § **418**.

32

*A SCENE OF CARNAGE**

At the kraal entrance the scene was a strange one. The slaughter was over by now, and the wounded men had been[1] put out of their pain, for no quarter had been given. The bush-closed entrance was trampled flat, and in place of bushes it was filled with the bodies of dead men. Dead men, everywhere dead men—they lay about in knots, they were flung by ones and twos in every position upon the open spaces, for all the world like the people on[2] the grass in one of the London parks on[3] a particularly hot Sunday in August. In front of this entrance, on a space which had been cleared of dead and of the shields and spears which were scattered in all directions as they had fallen or been thrown from the hands of their owners, stood and lay[4] the survivors of the awful struggle, and at their feet were four wounded men. We had gone into the fight thirty strong, and of the thirty but fifteen remained alive, and five of them (including Mr Mackenzie) were wounded, two mortally. Of those who held the entrance, Curtis and the Zulu alone remained. Good had lost five men killed, I had lost two killed, and Mackenzie no less than five out of the six with him. As for the survivors they were, with the exception of myself who had never come to close quarters, red from head to foot—Sir Henry's armour might have been painted that colour—and utterly exhausted, except Umslopogaas, who, as he grimly stood on a little mound above a heap of dead, leaning[5] as usual upon his axe, did not seem particularly distressed, although the skin over the hole in his head palpitated violently.

H. RIDER HAGGARD:

Allan Quatermain (Longmans, Green, 1887)

[1] Use the active voice. [2] *i.e.*, "people lying on." [3] § **286**. 1.

[4] Translate: "standing or lying" and place towards the beginning of the sentence, using a stock verb such as *se trouver* at this point.

[5] § **116**. *Note* (*c*).

33

*A FOX-HUNT***

Soon we turned in at some lodge gates, crossed the corner of an undulating park, and then everyone pulled up outside a belt of brown woodland. The hounds had disappeared, but I could hear the huntsman's voice a little way off. He was making noises which I identified as not altogether unlike those I had read about in Surtees. After a time the chattering crowd of riders moved slowly into the wood which appeared to be a large one.

My first reaction to the 'field' was one of mute astonishment. I had taken it for granted that there would be people 'in pink,' but these enormous confident strangers overwhelmed my mind with the visible authenticity of their brick-red coats. It all felt quite different to reading Surtees by the schoolroom fire.

But I was too shy to stare about me, and every moment I was expecting an outburst[1] of mad excitement in which I should find myself galloping wildly out of the wood. When the outbreak of activity came I had no time to think about it. For no apparent reason the people around me (we were moving[2] slowly along a narrow path in the wood) suddenly set off at a gallop and for several minutes I was aware of nothing but the breathless flurry of being carried along, plentifully spattered with mud by the sportsman in front of me. Suddenly, without any warning, he pulled up. Sheila automatically followed suit, shooting me well up her neck. The next moment everyone turned round and we all went tearing back by the way we had come. I found Dixon in front of me now, and he turned his head with a grin of encouragement.

SIEGFRIED SASSOON:

Memoirs of a Fox-hunting Man (Faber and Faber, 1928)

[1] Can be turned by a verb.

[2] A more suitable order for the French sentence would be, "While we were moving . . . the people around me."

34

*A SENTIMENTAL APPRAISAL*****

This time he dipped the oars very slowly indeed; and, while for a period that was longer than it seemed to them they floated vaguely, they mainly sat and glowed at each other as if everything had been settled. There were reasons enough why Nick should be happy; but it is a singular fact that the leading one was the sense of his having escaped a great and ugly mistake. The final result of his mother's appeal to him the day before had been the idea that he must act with unimpeachable honour. He was capable of taking it as an assurance that Julia had placed him under an obligation a gentleman could regard but in one way. If she herself had understood it so, putting the vision, or at any rate the appreciation, of a closer tie into everything she had done for him, the case was conspicuously simple and his course unmistakably plain. That is why he had been gay when he came out of the house to look for her: he could be gay when his course was plain. He could be all the gayer, naturally, I must add, that, in turning things over as he had done half the night, what he had turned up oftenest was the recognition that Julia now had a new personal power with him. It was not for nothing that she had thrown herself personally into his life. She had by her act made him live twice as intensely, and such an office, such a service, if a man had accepted and deeply tasted it, was certainly a thing to put him on his honour. He took it as distinct that there was nothing he could do in preference that wouldn't be spoiled for him by any deflection from that point. His mother had made him uncomfortable by bringing it so heavily up that Julia was in love with him—he didn't like in general to be told such things; but the responsibility seemed easier to carry and he was less shy about it when once he was away from other eyes, with only Julia's own to express that truth and with indifferent nature all about. Besides, what discovery had he made this morning but that he also was in love?

HENRY JAMES:
The Tragic Muse (Macmillan, 1921)

35

*TEACHING GAMES TO AN APE****

Anyhow, I was interested to see how far my Stamboul ape would get. Its chess was only moderate, because, as I said earlier, it copied all my moves. I wondered how much it understood of the moves and their consequences, but it would take my pieces as I took its pieces, and remove them from the board. It really seemed more at home with draughts, and also played a quite good snakes and ladders, but was furious when it came to a snake and had to go back. When it was angry, and particularly at croquet, a game which engendered in it as much fury as it does in other beings, it set up a great gibbering and chattering, and whenever it could it cheated. As I was trying to start it in moral sense, I spoke to it very sharply about this, and put on its collar and chain as a punishment, but I was not sure if it fully understood. As a partner it was very good; we would play together against Meg with her two balls, and it had a very precise aim and powerful force; all I had to do was to indicate what ball it was to make for, and it would hit it from any distance and send it to the other end of the lawn. Sometimes we played tennis, and at this it was better still, it had a very fine overhand service and a tremendous volley from the back line, and when it hit me on the head with the ball it was because it had tried to. It was an excitable player, dancing about and somersaulting in triumph when it had sent an untakable return, throwing its racket at the net when it had missed a ball, and pelting its opponent with balls with the strength with which its ancestors had no doubt flung coconuts at their enemies in their native jungles. A little more training in etiquette and sportsmanship, and it would easily qualify for Wimbledon. I saw no reason why there should not be an apes' four and singles, which would bring in a wonderful gate.

ROSE MACAULAY:

The Towers of Trebizond (Collins, 1956)

36

*AN UNEXPECTED PRESENT**

The sound of a truck pulling up to the house awakened him. Barefooted, he crept halfway down the stairs and crouched there, watching and waiting. A key turned in the lock and the next instant the lower floor and the kitchen were flooded with light.

"Boy?" her voice called softly.

He made no sound. She came to the stairs and saw him

crouching there. "Come down, boy," she said. "I brought[1] you something."

Tempted, he came slowly down the steps and she placed the long paper envelope in his arms. His fingers tore at the string and tape. The paper fell away. The entire world lay in his hands: a fishing rod as beautiful as any in Mr Johnson's boat, all gleaming steel and shining guides and wondrous nickelled reel; out of the bottom of the package fell an ivory spool wound with black thread line and last of all two lures, one with yellow and grey feathers, the other shining silver with wavering red and white paint on its back.

Incoherent words tumbled from his throat. He dropped to the floor flat on his stomach and lined his gifts up in front of him, touching each one with idolising fingers. He put the rod together, then took it apart, then started the whole procedure all over again. Once he tossed a remark at the woman in the rocker and for an instant saw her face; he had a sense that the eyes behind the spectacles were filled with tears, but then he forgot it in his engrossment. The universe lay on the floor beside him. The kitchen was no more; it had become the far reaches of the blue lake.

HOWARD MAIER:
"The Bridge" from *World Prize Stories* (Odhams, 1952)

[1] The simple past tense is an Americanism.

37

*A STORM***

The flash lit the eastern rooms of the house in the forest, and the girl in the gallery above the hall cried to the woman sitting[1] by the hearth below:

"Mother, Mother, did you see that light?"

The answer of the mother was lost in the clashing-to of a door upon the landing, and another door downstairs. A wind was rushing through every chink and crack and keyhole in the southern face of the house. The daughter took a step towards her mother's bedroom door, in order to close the window, when another but lesser flash lit the wall opposite. Thunder crashed immediately. There was a third flash and crash, and the baying of the hound by the fire. A storm of hail drove against the window. The girl forced open the door, and with difficulty closed the lattice. Her face and hands tingled with the beat of the icy fragments, some of which[2] were nearly as big as acorns.

As she ran down the staircase a rolling detonation shook the walls, and her mother at the foot of the stairs cried out her name: "Mamis!"

The girl jumped the last four stairs, and ran to her side. Her mother was pale, and Mamis was alarmed.

Hailstones were coming down the chimney and hissing in the flames of oak logs. The wind raved at door and window; flames and smoke poured out of the hearth into the room; flakes of ash settled on the hair of the mother sitting in an armchair, and on Mamis kneeling[1] by her anxiously.

HENRY WILLIAMSON:

The Star-Born (Faber and Faber, 1948)

[1] § **116**. *Note* (*c*). [2] § **207**. *Notes*.

38

*CATCHING A BUS***

A rapping on glass made him turn round.[1] An old lady and a big parrot were glaring at him from a ground-floor window. He bowed deeply, then remembered his bus and ran out on to the pavement. A couple of hundred yards away[2] a bus was coming slowly up the hill from the city.[3] It was too far off for him to[4] be able to read its destination screen, and in any case his exertions had misted his glasses over. But it must[5] be the one and he must get it. He sensed, as far as he could sense anything at the moment, that something would go badly wrong if he failed to turn up at the station, that something he wanted would be withdrawn. He began running even faster, so that people began to skip out of his way and look at him with wondering resentment. The bus, unable for the moment to begin its turn into College Road, was halted in mid-traffic and was, he could now see, his bus. He ran steadily towards the corner of College Road, but the bus began moving again and reached it before him. When he next saw the bus, it was halted about fifty yards away up College Road,[6] and someone had just got on.

Dixon broke into a frenzied, lung-igniting[7] sprint, while the conductor watched him immobile from the platform. When he was halfway to the bus, this official rang the bell, the driver let in the clutch, and the wheels began to turn. Dixon found he was even better at running than he'd thought, but when the gap between man and bus had narrowed to perhaps five yards, it began to widen[8] rapidly.

KINGSLEY AMIS:
Lucky Jim (Gollancz, 1954)

[1] § **92**. 4. [2] § **282**. 1. (*b*).
[3] Translate: "a bus coming from the city" etc.
[4] § **387**. [5] § **83**. 3., § **84**. 1.
[6] Translate: "in College road, fifty yards away."
[7] An adverbial expression with *à* might be used. See § **102**. 2. (*b*).
[8] Add "again."

39

*EPISODE IN A WALKING TOUR****

The entomologist went off for an hour with our white-bearded guide—white-bearded, leather-faced, black-eyed like an animal, seventy-three years old—while I slept for an hour by a cold spring, after a drink and bathing[1] of tired feet. It was on the way back I saw my plant and all that went with it, on[2] the sore twenty miles towards the end of a day which out of stillness and exhilarating sunshine had shaped a howling, dust-raising gale. The knobble stones slipped away under my automatic feet on[3] the nearly perpendicular slope of the last mile. The dust drove up into my face, my nose was crimson, my face and hands walnut. But I remember nothing of that without an effort, nothing or next to nothing of the feel of my face, the tiredness, the unstable slope; and I should have forgotten it if I had not made notes the same evening. But the plant, as I say, was planted there and then in my mind. It was on the plateau between the mountain and the first miles[4] of descent towards Aritzo. We had passed a valley down which a forest of vast, squat, wide oak trees was visible a mile or two miles away. It was like a drawing in one of Edward Lear's Mediterranean travel books. I looked at the darkness between the trunks through field-glasses and knew, reluctantly, that I should never walk in among them. Then, on the path which was now clear we came to a grove of very old, twisted holly trees, which thickened from their base, narrowed, and thickened again, and were frilled with branch holes and hollows. I have seen hollies like them in the moisture of north Somerset against the Bristol Channel, and in the Lake District. A dog jumped up, ears back, snarling between visible teeth. Our guide threw it a crust from[5] his haversack. Then, among the hollies, a shepherd; and around the shepherd and around the holly trees stem after stem, flower after flower (though many of them were in seed) of a wild peony, a white peony. The hollies were dark, the peonies were light; and light against the shepherd, hooded and cloaked in black wool.

GEOFFREY GRIGSON:

Places of the Mind (Routledge and Kegan Paul, 1949)

[1] "drink," "bathing of": use verbs.

[2] Translate by a phrase, *e.g.*: "while covering."

[3] The English will have to be modified for the purpose of translation: *e.g.*, "while I was covering the last mile of the path which rose almost perpendicularly."

[4] Is the term of measurement essential here? If not, the English means "the first part of the slope that leads down."

[5] "which he took from."

DESCRIPTIVE

40

*AN INTERIOR*****

We walked through a high hallway into a bright rosy-coloured space, fragilely bound into the house by french windows at either end. The windows were ajar and gleaming white against the fresh grass outside that seemed to grow a little way into the house. A breeze blew through the room, blew curtains in at one end and out the other like pale flags, twisting them up toward the frosted wedding-cake of the ceiling, and then rippled over the wine-coloured rug, making a shadow on it as wind does on the sea.

The only completely stationary object in the room was an enormous couch on which two young women were buoyed up as though upon an anchored balloon. They were both in white, and their dresses were rippling and fluttering as if they had just been blown back in after a short flight around the house. I must have stood for a few moments listening to the whip and snap of the curtains and the groan of a picture on the wall. Then there was a boom as Tom Buchanan shut the rear windows and the caught wind died out about the room and the curtains and the rugs and the two young women ballooned slowly to the floor.

The younger of the two was a stranger to me. She was extended full length at her end of the divan, completely motionless, and with her chin raised a little, as if she were balancing something on it which was quite likely to fall. If she saw me out of the corner of her eyes she gave no hint of it—indeed, I was almost surprised into murmuring an apology for having disturbed her by coming in.

The other girl Daisy, made an attempt to rise—she leaned slightly forward with a conscientious expression—then she laughed, an absurd, charming little laugh, and I laughed too and came forward into the room.

F. Scott Fitzgerald:
The Great Gatsby (Chatto and Windus, 1926)

41

*SNOW IN ROME**

I pulled aside the curtain and saw that snow was falling over Rome, flickering in the light of its lamps, whitening the streets and settling softly on arch and pillar.[1] The most dignified city in Europe was transformed suddenly into a city of urchins. A man in an opera hat on his way to the Constanza Theatre picked up a handful of snow which he pretended to throw at his friend. He did not instinctively make a hard ball of it as any northern man would have done:[2] he just picked up the softness and threw it in the air where the wind blew and scattered it.

And I remembered what it was like when we were children to awaken in the night and see snow falling on tree and field.[1] How exciting it was. How exquisitely the snow transformed a well-known world. It was as though the earth, in tune with our youth, was 'dressing up' for a charade.

I went out into the streets where flakes spun and whirled in the night. All Rome was out of doors marvelling[3] at it. It seemed to me so strange that[4] a city which has known so much should be so moved by snowflakes.

I came upon a group of elderly Romans solemnly rolling an enormous snowball down the Capitoline Hill. Even the wolves in the cage beneath the Capitol sat on their haunches with their muzzles against the wire-netting watching the strange thing that had happened to their city.

H. V. MORTON:

Blue Days at Sea (Methuen, 1932)

[1] Use plurals and definite articles. [2] § **223**. [3] § **99**. [4] § **379**.

42

*THE DAILY ROUND**

I go then to the cupboard, and take[1] the damp bags of rich sultanas; I lift the heavy flour on to the clean scrubbed kitchen table. I knead; I stretch; I pull, plunging my hands in the warm inwards of the dough. I let the cold water stream fanwise through my fingers. The fire roars; the flies buzz in a circle. All my currants and rices, the silver bags and the blüe bags, are locked again in the cupboard. The meat is stood in the oven; the bread rises in a soft dome under the clean towel. I walk in the afternoon down to the river. All the world is[2] breeding. The flies are going from grass to grass. The flowers are thick with pollen. The swans ride the stream in order. The clouds, warm now, sun-spotted, sweep over the hills, leaving gold in the water, and gold on the necks of the swans. Pushing one foot before the other, the cows munch their way across[3] the field. I feel through[4] the grass for[5] the white-domed mushroom; and break its stalk and pick the purple orchid that grows beside it and lay the orchid by the mushroom with the earth at its root, and so home to make the kettle boil for my father among the just reddened roses on the tea-table.

But evening comes and the lamps are lit. And when evening comes and the lamps are lit they make a yellow fire in the ivy. I sit with my sewing by the table. I think of Jinny; of Rhoda; and hear the rattle of wheels on the pavement as the farm horses plod home; I hear traffic roaring[6] in the evening wind. I look at the quivering leaves in the dark garden and think: "They dance in London. Jinny kisses Louis."

VIRGINIA WOOLF:

The Waves (The Hogarth Press, 1931)

[1] § **229**. (*a*). [2] § **73**. 5. *Note* (*a*).

[3] Translate "across" by a verb, "munch" by an explanatory phrase.

[4] "feel through"—*i.e.*, "pass (slide) my hand through."

[5] Clarify by a phrase, *e.g.*, "in order to pick."

[6] Translate: "the roaring of the traffic" and arrange the rest of the sentence accordingly.

43

*AN INTERESTING GHOST**

I must explain that I departed this life nearly five years ago. But I did not altogether depart this world. There were those odd things still to be done which one's executors can never do properly. Papers to be looked over, even after[1] the executors have torn them up. Lots of business except, of course, on Sundays[2] and Holidays of Obligation, plenty to take an interest in for the time being. I take my recreation on Saturday mornings. If it is a wet Saturday I wander up and down the substantial lanes of Woolworth's as I did[3] when I was young and visible. There is a pleasurable spread of objects on the counters which I now perceive and exploit with a certain detachment, since it suits with my condition of life. Creams, toothpastes, combs and hankies, cotton gloves, flimsy flowering scarves, writing-paper and crayons, ice-cream cones and orangeade, screwdrivers, boxes of tacks, tins of paint, of glue, of marmalade; I always like them, but far more now that I have no need of any. When Saturdays are fine I go instead to the Portobello Road where formerly I would jaunt with Kathleen in our grown-up days. The barrow-loads do not change much, of apples and rayon vests in common blues and low-taste mauve, of silver plate, trays and teapots long since changed hands from the bygone citizens to dealers, from shops to the new flats and breakable homes, then over to the barrow-stalls and the dealers again: Georgian spoons, rings, ear-rings of turquoise and opal set in the butterfly pattern or true-lovers' knot, patch-boxes with miniature paintings of ladies on ivory, snuff-boxes of silver with Scotch pebbles inset.

MURIEL SPARK:
"The Portobello Road" from *Winter's Tales II* (Macmillan, 1956)

[1] § **385**. [2] § **168**. 5. [3] § **223**.

44

*LONDON WINTER*****

Though the air was stinging, his circulation was so well able to resist it that he could enjoy the beauties of Nature as wholeheartedly, as if he were walking on a June afternoon; and indeed they deserved enjoyment. "It can all be done in one single line," winter was saying of the trees, "if one is careful to keep the point of the pen on the paper, and charges it discreetly with the Indian Ink. And line, of course, is the thing.

But it cannot be done this way unless you choose a good solid dull sky as a background. You will be driven to the weak, water-colour methods of my poor sister Spring if you confuse your background with dots and dashes of sunshine; and if you flood it with a gross plenitude of blue as Summer does, then there is nothing for it but to go in for her shapeless and strong-coloured flummery of leaves. And if you let all get sodden with gold, as Autumn does, then there is nothing for it but to paint like Turner and be damned. But if you care for line, why here it is."

And there it was, on each side of the road through Hyde Park, in black traceries on dun that made the human attempts at acuity in the form of the spiked railings below seem bluntness itself; and yet further off, out of the foreground of the eye, where they marked the course of the Ladies' Mile and Rotten Row, they melted into a lacey darkness soft as soot.

Because the grass beneath them was brindled with light snow, this darkness seemed intense to the point of vehemence. Now that the earth itself had taken on the colour of old age, the tree-trunks themselves, which at other times are the least spectacular forms of growth, created a feeling of resolute increase such as is given ordinarily by some prodigious show of leaf or flower or fruit. They might have been black flames thrusting upwards through the effete soil, from some subterranean powerhouse far too fierce to paint them with the ruddy hues that belong to fires of a more superficial kindling.

The scene, rich as it was in spite of being crowded with signs of the suspension of all opulence, suggested a plutonic energy working exultantly in spite of the lack of these encouragements which man considers necessary to sweeten his toil.

That impression grew stronger as there thundered along the riding-track beside him a party of horsemen whose faces were contracted with pain at the bitterness of the air, and yet were magnificent with pride at their government of their mounts and pleasure in the speed to which they compelled them. It increased his already enormous satisfaction with the afternoon that not for more than a minute did he feel that cringing resentment which those who walk commonly feel at the sight of those who ride, since he could remind himself that now he was among the riders, and had himself often caused others to cringe.

REBECCA WEST:
Harriet Hume (Hutchinson, 1937)

45

*NATURE'S PENDULUM***

Suddenly I have sensed the approach of midsummer. It is as though I had surprised the stealthy advance and taken time unawares. Overnight the blossom has gone from the hedgerows, the roadside fringes of chervil have turned brown, meadows and hedge elms have become dense and dark, the buttercup gold is past its best. Most conclusive proof was the first sight of a dog rose on the second of June and many more today (the fifth) and I notice that an elder bush which grows beside my potting shed is knotting up for bloom. The elder is virtually the last conspicuous hedgerow shrub to flower and the limes are also the last trees to bloom.

I do not like to be reminded of the progress of the summer so sharply, the swing of nature's pendulum is more poignant[1] than that of a clock, it tells me that my own life is ticking away too fast. I cannot explain why it is that as we grow older, day by day, time seems to increase its pace. I have no wish to be hurried like this, willy nilly, through such a wondrous world. I must say that since I have become a man of so-called leisure, free to live my life to my own liking, time does not seem to run away quite so fast. It was appalling, a few years back, to be aware of each season passing[2] ever more swiftly, of young friends growing up with the rapidity of hedgerow plants. One moment they would be grubby and timorous Lower School boys, the next young men going out into the world, altered so oddly by manhood, all so courteous, friendly, well-mannered. With frightening speed those terms reeled by me. I had few friends among the Staff but very many among the boys, especially those whose tastes were my tastes, birds and sport. Even the summer terms with their long evenings, when the ringing 'tap tap' of cricket balls at the nets was part of summer, passed as quickly as the winter terms when, at Last Lesson, the clatter of feet and hum of voices passed along the lamplit street.

'BB':

Letters from Compton Deverell (Eyre and Spottiswoode, 1950)

[1] Probably clearer to add "to me." [2] *Qui. cf.* § **115.** 2.

46

*THE GARDEN SEAT**

There had never been a proper seat in the garden, and so[1] at last, in a country sale, they bought one. It had recently been re-painted white, and it was quite a nice piece of work, solid and well-shaped. For protection against wind they stood it in the sunken rockery, where it blocked half the path, necessitating a slight detour. For further shelter an embankment was made at the back of the seat, and for prettiness' sake they planted yellow alyssum along the top of the bank.

It looked attractive in its new white paint.[2] Occasionally someone would sit on it to read or write, or a child would use it as a boat, but none of these things happened at all often, as it still seemed much more natural to sit on the stone steps, to lie on the grass and to go sailing in a construction of deck-chairs.

After the first year the long grass on the bank began to poke through the slats of the back, and the alyssum, a vigorous and fast-growing plant, to hang down over the centre of it. By July[3] it was only possible to sit at the ends; towards the middle the plants tickled, and it was a pity to crush them. Starting with coin-like pieces over the knots in the wood, the paint flaked a little then cracked along the lines of the grain. Before being painted white for the sale, the seat had been green, and before that again it had received a coat of brown varnish.

JACQUETTA HAWKES:
Fables (The Cresset Press, 1953)

[1] **§ 344**.
[2] A more natural version can be obtained by changing the order: "its new coat of white paint. . . ."
[3] "Already in July."

47

*PRELUDE TO A RAILWAY JOURNEY*****

Even when he had bought his ticket, a first-class that he could hardly afford, in the leisurely fashion demanded by such an act of self-indulgence, and had loitered at the kiosks buying papers and a tin of tobacco, Adam Stewart discovered that he had still some twenty minutes or so left. Not that it mattered; they would soon pass. He found himself repeating, with the solemn relish of one who achieves nonsense, "Pancrastination is the thief of time." St Pancras, surely the most canonical of all our stations, seemed to rebuke his levity. Indignant puffs of smoke and steam, sudden red glares of anger, ascended to the great arched roof. The locomotives grunted and wheezed like outraged sacristans. The thin high voices of the newsboys ran together into a protesting chorus of virgins and elders. But no, that was Greek drama, Adam reminded himself, and nothing to do with cathedrals, and it is with cathedrals that large railway stations must always be compared. He strolled towards his train, waiting there with a long perspective of open doors, and for a moment or so enjoyed the feeling of large and superior leisure that visits the traveller who has time to spare, and watched other and less fortunate passengers, scurrying here and there, dwindling into agitated pigmies before his calm gaze. But he found it impossible to enjoy anything else, although there were so many things he ought to be enjoying. He ought to be hugging the promise of the coming journey, and the thought of the little holiday, tossed out of the blue, to which it was the rattling overture. He had always rapturously anticipated such things before—indeed, that had always been the best part of it—but this time nothing was happening.

There, where the great dim cave ended, was the blazing June sunshine, and beyond the few miles of hot bricks outside were the fields that would tear past him hour after hour, scribbling their zig-zag gold and white lines of buttercups and daisies.

J. B. Priestley:
Adam in Moonshine (Heinemann, 1927)

48

*ASHEHAM HOUSE***

The bottom meadow, in which Asheham stands, lay between high banks, on the slopes of which[1] grew tall beech trees, and ran back into the main mass of Itford hill which rose from the farmyard behind the house to a height of five hundred feet. Asheham itself looked west across the river valley to Rodmell, a mile or so away on the first high ground on the other side of the water meadows. It has a plain front and a slate roof, but its most striking feature is its fenestration: double french windows with arched lights over them: the combination gives its façade a curiously dreamlike character, like a house drawn on a plate or by[2] a child. Asheham was a little set apart, not quite of the real world, like the houses in Walter de la Mare's novels. It was haunted, though I never saw a ghost. Clive (the most unlikely of all the rationalists who stayed or lived in it in company with Duncan and Harry Norton) did actually see a ghost: a figure passing from room to room and crossing the windows, as they walked up to the house when they knew for a fact that it was empty. They found it empty when they went in. Virginia wrote *A Haunted House* in the collection of experimental sketches and impressions which she published in *Monday or Tuesday*, a year or two after the visit I shall describe, and that lovely sketch evokes the ghost of Asheham, a house with a personal character as individual as that of a woman one has loved, and who is dead. For many years Asheham house has only been a ghost, for though it is standing its surroundings have been utterly transformed. An immense heap of spoilage has been dumped into the flat meadow in front of it, entirely shutting out the view. This[3] is now overgrown with briars and bushes and young trees. Huge sheds, warehouses and a roasting oven with a tall chimney fill the old farmyard. Much of the down behind has been excavated. The great yellow lorries grind up[4] to it empty along[5] a wide concrete roadway and rumble away with loads of cement in paper bags.

DAVID GARNETT:

Flowers of the Forest (Chatto and Windus, 1955)

[1] § **207**. *Note* (*a*).

[2] Use another participle to carry on the idea of "drawn."

[3] Specify in the translation.

[4] Translate "up" by a verb. Use a descriptive phrase to bring out the force of "grind."

[5] *sur*.

49

*LONDON TRAFFIC***

There were two techniques to deal with the problem of getting in or out of London between six and seven on a summer evening. One was to trickle gently along, keeping a uniform distance from the man in front, stopping when he stopped and starting when he started instead of at the amber light, keeping your finger off[1] the horn and your eye off the clock, worrying not, because if you were late, you were late and, short of fitting a gyrocopter device to your car and lifting it out of the ruck, there was nothing you could do about it. The other way was to rush up as close as possible to the car in front and then jam on your brakes, changing down immediately and keeping the clutch almost engaged, quivering under your foot like an eager horse, so that you could shoot forward as soon as the other man, stung by your horn, moved ponderously on. Steven favoured the latter method. At least it gave the illusion of speed.

As[2] he crawled and stopped and started and darted into

momentary gaps, Steven found himself planning[3] his evening over and over again, making a mental[4] timetable of his visits, judging how soon he could be home. Ten minutes for putting the car away; dinner, with the evening paper and that article of Blanchard's on burns which he had been meaning to read for the last three days; cigarette, listen to the news, then into his consulting-room and get out the typewriter and the big crammed blotter with the picture of[5] what looked like the Duke of Windsor in a top hat, jumping a six-barred gate on a yellow horse.

MONICA DICKENS:
Thursday Afternoons (Michael Joseph, 1945)

[1] Translate: "taking care not to touch." [2] § **410**. 3.
[3] *Cf.* § **73**. 5. *Note* (*a*). § **99**. 1. [4] Best translated by an adverb.
[5] Use a verb, *e.g.*, "represent."

50

*A MOUNTAIN LANDSCAPE*****

The irregular meadows run in and out like inlets of lakes among these harvested rocks, sweet with perpetual streamlets, that seem always to have chosen the steepest places to come down, for the sake of the leaps, scattering their handfuls of crystal this way and that, as the wind takes them, with all the grace, but with none of the formalism of fountains; dividing into fanciful change of dash and spring, yet with the seal of their granite channels upon them, as the lightest play of human speech may bear the seal of past toil; and closing back out of their spray to lave the rigid angles and brighten with silver fringes and glassy films each lower and lower step of sable stone; until at last, gathered altogether again, except, perhaps, some chance drops caught on the apple-blossom, where it had budded a little nearer the cascade than it did last spring—they find their way down to the turf, and lose themselves in that, silently, with quiet depth of clear water furrowing among the grass blades, and looking only like their shadow, but presently emerging again in little startled gushes and laughing hurries, as if they had remembered suddenly that the day was too short for them to get down the hill.

Green fields and glowing rock, and glancing streamlet, all slope together in the sunshine towards the brows of the ravines, where the pines take up their own dominion of saddened shade, and with everlasting roar in the twilight the stronger torrents thunder down pale from the glaciers, filling all their chasms with enchanted cold, beating themselves to pieces against the great rocks that they have themselves cast down, and forcing fierce way beneath their ghastly poise.

The mountain paths stoop to these glens in forky zigzags, leading to some grey and narrow arch, all fringed under its shuddering curve with the ferns that fear the light, a cross of rough-hewn pine, iron-bound to its parapet, standing dark against the lurid fury of the foam. Far up the glen, as we pause beside the cross, the sky is seen through the openings in the pines, thin with excess of light; and in its clear consuming flame of white space, the summits of the rocky mountains are gathered into solemn crowns and circlets, all flushed in that strange, faint silence of possession by the sunshine which has in it so deep a melancholy; full of power, yet as frail as shadows; lifeless, like the walls of a sepulchre, yet beautiful in tender fall of crimson folds, like the veil of some sea spirit, that lives and dies as the foam flashes; fixed on a perpetual throne; stern against all strength, lifted above all sorrow, and yet effaced and melted utterly into the air by that last sunbeam that has crossed to them from between the two golden clouds.

JOHN RUSKIN:
Modern Painters

51

*LONDON AND PARIS, 1877****

With the advance of the spring and the development of the season, in London, the streets (in the West End) begin to present to the eye of an observant stranger a great many new characteristics. The dusky metropolis takes on, here and there, in spots, a perceptible brightness, and as the days elapse these spots increase and multiply. At last they produce a general impression of brilliancy. Thanks to this combined effect, the murky Babylon by the Thames becomes cheerful and splendid. At the climax of the season, of a fine, fresh day in June, the West End exhibits a radiance which, to my sense, casts into the shade even the charming brightness of Paris. The brightness of Paris is, as I say, charming; it is a very pretty spectacle; it flashes and twinkles, and laughs, and murmurs. Stand on the edge of the Place de la Concorde, at the bottom of the Champs-Élysées, on any fine-weathered Sunday in the late spring—on a day when there are races beyond the Bois de Boulogne—and you will feel the full force of all the traditions about Paris being the gayest, easiest, eagerest, most pleasure-taking of capitals. The light has a silvery shimmer, the ladies' dresses in the carriages a charming harmony, the soldiers' red trousers a martial animation, the white caps of the *bonnes* a gleaming freshness. The carriages sweep in a dense line up the long vista of the Champs-Élysées, amid the cool, fresh verdure, and the lines of well-dressed people sitting on neat little yellow chairs; the great mass of the Arc de Triomphe rises with majestic grace, transmuted by distance into a sort of violet shadow; the fountains sparkle and drizzle in the vast sunny *place*; the Seine sweeps by in an amber flood, through a channel that gleams like marble beneath the league-long frontage of the splendid Louvre, and beyond that, crowning the picturesque purple mass before which the river divides, the towers of Notre-Dame stand up and balance in the opposite distance with the softened majesty of the Arch.

HENRY JAMES:

"The Picture Season in London" from *Galaxy* of August 1877

52

*HEARTH AND HOME***

When I seek in the depths of memory those early childhood feelings, visiting rooms I once knew, I see first of all the fire. I always stand on the threshold of a doorway and look at the fire. Then I go forward in imagination and everything is remembered[1] with a glow upon it, darkly shadowed or candle-lit, but lighted by the fire on the hearth, which burned[2] winter and summer. Little attics that had no fireplace, barns and stables, cowhouses and sheds, all are seen in exact detail as if a photograph had been taken at some unknown time, but I do not linger. I hurry down the stone stairways, I fling open a door and gaze hungrily at the fire which gives life to the house. This visual image is so clear, I am warmed as I raise it out of the depths and enter a life once lived. Then illuminated faces come from the shadows and people welcome me and I am free to wander wherever I desire.

There was the kitchen fire, the most royal and grand, tended with religious care, for it was the core of the house. Upon its heat might depend life and death. Fire meant hot water in the sudden emergencies of[3] a farm, it meant warmth for a sick animal, and a chilled man whose heart was frozen. On the broad hearthstone, sanded to a rich golden yellow with a lump of stone from the hill, and kept immaculately clean, the flames beat down with life-giving strength. The round plaited basket with a sickly chicken lay there, covered with a cloth, or a bird someone had found hurt, or a newborn lamb weak and struggling for new life, or dough rising in a yellow pancheon. All were given life. Close to the hearth sat the man who had come home from a journey white-lipped[4] after driving in the icy winds, eyes blinking back the water. Snow and frost, wild gales and heavy rain, all might do their worst, but there was that glorious fire to think of during the long drive home.

ALISON UTTLEY:

Plowmen's Clocks (Faber and Faber, 1952)

[1] "is seen again in memory."

[2] Add "there."

[3] Translate by a phrase, *e.g.*, "which often arise."

[4] Nominative absolute in French. See § **178**. *Cp*. § **282**. 3 (*c*).

53

*A SUCCESSFUL POET****

Peaceful is the first word which a house agent would have chosen in describing the home of Philip Ploss. Ancient and unpretentious, with its modern conveniences tucked unobtrusively away and even its excellent state of repair modestly dissimulated, Lark Manor nestled in the heart of the English countryside. The railway station was five minutes' walk from the house and quite concealed; from it the fastest trains—and the fastest were so very fast that it was wonderful how very smooth they were, too—took just half an hour to reach London.

The distance was right. In half an hour, and while hurtling towards the pleasures of his club and a matinée and dinner with a female friend, Philip Ploss could comfortably write fifteen to twenty lines of verse. These verses, which sometimes concerned the delight of travelling in a smooth train from the squalor of the city to the pleasures of a rural retreat, he would leave at his club for one or another of his acquaintances who ran a literary magazine. And two or three weeks later they would be printed and there would be a cheque which paid for the matinée and the dinner, with maybe a little over for other things. And then every three or four years all these verses would be collected in a slim volume by another acquaintance, a publisher. Philip Ploss incurred no expense whatever and there was a deferred royalty which had several times come to over five pounds. This, together with a couple of thousand or so a year which Ploss had inherited from a father in tea, helped to maintain the notable peacefulness of Lark.

MICHAEL INNES:
The Secret Vanguard (Gollancz, 1940)

54

*A STRICT COMMUNITY***

Pacific Grove and Monterey sit side by side on a hill bordering the bay. The two towns touch shoulders but they are not alike. Whereas Monterey was founded a long time ago by foreigners, Indians and Spaniards and such, and the town grew up higgledy-piggledy without plan or purpose, Pacific Grove sprang full-blown from the iron heart of a psycho-ideo-legal religion. It was formed as a retreat in the 1880's and came fully equipped with laws, ideals and customs. On the town's statute books a deed is void if liquor is ever brought on the property. As a result, the sale of iron-and-wine tonic is fantastic. Pacific Grove has a law that requires you to pull your blinds down after sundown, and forbids you to pull them down before. Scorching on bicycles is forbidden as is sea-bathing and boating on Sundays. There is one crime which is not defined but which is definitely against the law. Hijinks are or is[1] forbidden. It must be admitted that most of these laws are not enforced to the hilt. The fence that once surrounded the Pacific Grove retreat is no longer in existence.

Once during its history Pacific Grove was in trouble, deep trouble. You see, when the town was founded many old people moved to the retreat, people you'd think didn't have anything to retreat from. These old people became grumpy after a while and got to interfering in everything and causing trouble, until a philanthropist named Deems presented the town with two roque courts.

Roque is a complicated kind of croquet, with narrow wickets and short-handled mallets. You play off the side-lines, like billiards. Very complicated, it is. They say it develops character.

JOHN STEINBECK:
Sweet Thursday (Heinemann, 1954)

[1] The linguistic quibble need not be repeated in the French.

55

*AN EMPTY EVENING****

Evening came clear and breathless. A wisp of fog trailed over a glassy sea and made a brownish band against the lemon-coloured sky on the horizon. Swallows flew far above. The light lingered, but a dim, blue haziness blurred the outlines of the old warehouses, the crumbling archway, the boats riding at anchor in slack water. Inside the ugly building that housed the social club, shadows gathered. Joe wandered restlessly around the deserted billiard-room, reluctant to switch on the light and acknowledge another day's end. Sheeted billiard-tables loomed shapelessly in the gloom.

He switched on the wireless and switched it off again before it uttered more than a crackle of static. He picked up a magazine and carried it to the window, twisting it in an attempt to catch the fading light, but the print swam before his eyes and he threw the magazine on a seat. He walked to the empty fireplace and stared at the dim, dusty trophies in their glass-case, its green baize faded to a streaky olive. He tapped his foot on the fender and listened to the dull ringing sound. There was nothing to hold his roving mind.

He began to whistle softly, until the tune turned into "The Boys of Fair Hill" and died away. He walked to the door, then, with his hand already on the light-switch, he paused for a moment, irresolute. The clock ticked away loudly in the stillness, then groaned and wheezed and struck nine. The sound sank into the shadows. Joe pulled open the door abruptly and went down the steps, to cool evening air and gravel that crunched underfoot.

MAURICE KENNEDY:
"Vladivostok" from *Winter's Tales II* (Macmillan, 1956)

56

*AN IMPRESSION OF PROVENCE***

There appeared before my eyes[1] another part of France, the Provençal village where I spend my summers, the crook in the high street where the men sit[2] at little tables with heads[3] bent sideways and downwards[4] as if they all had stiff necks, watching[5] the game of *boules* that incredibly goes on, parting and reassembling as the automobiles fly past, in the puddle-pocked, wheel-harassed roads. It is not a likeable game. It brings two kinds of unpleasantness[6] to the ear, for when the *boules* meet the spurting sound of their impact is like an exchange of rude remarks, and when they meet only with a little force, as must often happen in a game played on such a surface, that sound has the futile quality of feeble rudeness, of failure in an enterprise where even success would have meant nothing pleasant. And there comes from the onlookers never that tense yet languid cry, only a little more than a deep breath, which tells that a crowd is participating through attention in the peace of a beautiful movement: instead come praising, blaming "Ohs!" and "Ahs!" which show that they are not resting, that in this pastime there has not been lifted from them the human burden of discrimination and calculation, that load of pricking needles. It is, therefore, better as one passes to raise one's eyes to the great umbrella pine which is the steady roof to all the squint-sitting people, making out of a hundred branches, a million twigs, a form as single as a raindrop, casting a shadow as of an undivided substance.

REBECCA WEST:

The Strange Necessity (Jonathan Cape, 1928)

[1] Note that the scene is recollected, not real.

[2] Action or state?

[3] **§ 178.**

[4] *i.e.*, "eyes lowered towards the ground," "looking down at the ground."

[5] **§ 99.**

[6] "kinds of unpleasantness." Use a more concrete expression in the French: *e.g.*, "unpleasant sounds."

57

*DOWN ON THE ALLOTMENT*****

Even into late spring on the allotments the thick dirty brussels-sprout stalks wait rotting to be chopped up and dug in to feed future lettuces whose last yellow leaves (mixed with old dried blood) bring on the new green autumn tomatoes which, though they never ripen in the quickly fading summer, at least make chutney to mature through the winter. The small stakes of earth wait to be dug over to sweeten in the sun, each guarded by a shack of clapboard or tin, cracked glazed salvaged window-frames thrown together in midget conservatory or summer-house style a bit fancy and painted a bottle-green. Held together with iron bed-heads (their brass knobs long lost) and bound by chicken wire, the allotments drag shaggily down to a tired meadow, and at their lower end the grass is already over-run, grown high as your knee.

Lying down here you smell the rank weeds and watch the ants scamper out of the bombardment of your breath. Between the roots they hide and hatch their tiny plots for survival, and, as history goes to show, they survive. The small flies and the narrow creamy moths dart into their bushy pleasure-houses, do their business and drop dead unconcerned. You could be miles away from the rubbish-tip now officially full and closed down by the all-powerful council. You are far away (although not in an altogether different world) from the ramshackle studios once again empty, the recent whitewash already grubby in the bright spring light, the temporarily made-good ruins back in their natural ruined splendour, flaking gently to dust in the sun. No estate agent (no matter how high-class) could argue that the lower end of the allotments was anything but desirable building land.

WOLF MANKOWITZ:

My Old Man's a Dustman (André Deutsch, 1956)

58

*AN OLD HOUSE REVISITED****

As I went up the lane to[1] the house I looked for the old sign of things: smoke rising from the chimney; the old summer bird-scares, age-green hats on sticks and inside-out umbrellas and twirling shuttlecocks; scarecrows made up of odd legs of Silas's pants and bell-bottomed trousers and the housekeeper's ancient hat and chemises; the ladder in the late apple trees; the bonfire filling the garden and the spinney and the fields with smoke that hung in sweet-smelling clouds under the pines and the golden cherry leaves. I listened for the cluck of Silas's hens and the grunting and rooting of the solitary sow he had always kept in the black sty under the elderberries at the garden end.

But it was very quiet, oddly silent everywhere. I could hear nothing. And then, coming to the garden gate, I saw that the gate and the fence, rain-green and patterned with prints of orange fungus for as long as I could remember, had been neatly repaired and painted white. The effect was curiously sepulchral. But it did not trouble me. It was only when I saw, beyond the fence, the stump of a sawn-down apple tree, and then another, and then another of a cherry tree, and beyond that a wide empty space where the gooseberry trees had been, and beyond that another white fence in place of the old wild elderberry hedge, that I began to grow perturbed and finally angry. And for some minutes I stood there on the grass outside, helpless, staring[2] at the white fences, the empty garden, the sawn-off tree-trunks, the newly white-painted windows until suddenly I could bear it no longer.

H. E. Bates:

My Uncle Silas (Jonathan Cape, 1939)

[1] "that leads to"

[2] Adverbial infinitive. See § **99**. 1.

59

*MEMORIES OF HOME***

Once, following his father from Chatham to Devonport, they had lived in a cottage on the edge of the moors. In the succession of houses that Ralph had known, this one stood out with particular clarity because after[1] that house he had been sent away to school. Mummy had still been with them and Daddy had[2] come home every day. Wild ponies came to the stone wall at the bottom of the garden, and it had snowed. Just behind the cottage there was a sort of shed and you could lie up there, watching[3] the flakes swirl past.[4] You could see the damp spot where each flake died; then you could mark the first flake that lay down without melting and watch the whole ground turn white. You could go indoors when you were cold and look out of the window, past that bright copper kettle and the plate with the little blue men——.

When you went to bed there was a bowl of cornflakes with sugar and cream. And the books—they stood on the shelf by the bed, leaning[5] together[6] with always two or three laid flat on top because he had not bothered to put them back properly. They were dog-eared and scratched. There was the bright, shining one about Topsy and Mopsy that he never read because it was about two girls; there was the one about the Magician which you read with a kind of tied-down terror, skipping page twenty-seven with the awful picture of the spider; there was a book about people who had dug things up, Egyptian things; there was *The Boy's Book of Trains*, *The Boy's Book of Ships*. Vividly they came before him; he could[7] have reached up and touched them, could feel the weight and slow slide with which the *Mammoth Book for Boys* would come out and slither down.

. . . Everything was all right; everything was good-humoured and friendly.

WILLIAM GOLDING:

The Lord of the Flies (Faber and Faber, 1954)

[1] "when they left." See § **395** (sequence of tenses).

[2] Past perfect or past descriptive? *Cp.* § **80.** and § **75.**, § **76**.

[3] See § **99**. 1.

[4] "past": translate by a verb; "swirl": translate by a gerund.

[5] § **116**. 2. (*c*). [6] § **251**. 7. [7] "it seemed to him that" etc.

CRITICISM

60

*THE BUSINESS OF CRITICISM*****

No doubt (as I have admitted) a philosophic training might possibly—ideally would—make a critic surer and more penetrating in the perception of significance and relation and in the judgment of value. But it is to be noted that the improvement we ask for is of the critic, the critic as critic, and to count on it would be to count on the attainment of an arduous ideal. It would be reasonable to fear—to fear blunting of edge, blurring of focus and muddled misdirection of attention: consequences of queering one discipline with the habits of another. The business of the literary critic is to attain a peculiar completeness of response and to observe a peculiarly strict relevance in developing his response into commentary; he must be on his guard against abstracting improperly from what is in front of him and against any premature or irrelevant generalising—of it or from it. His first concern is to enter into possession of the given poem (let us say) in its concrete fulness, and his constant concern is never to lose his completeness of possession, but rather to increase it. In making value-judgments (and judgments as to significance), implicitly or explicitly, he does so out of that completeness of possession and with that fulness of response. He doesn't ask, "How does this accord with these specifications of goodness in poetry?"; he aims to make fully conscious and articulate the immediate sense of value that 'places' the poem.

Of course, the process of 'making fully conscious and articulate' is a process of relating and organising, and the 'immediate sense of value' should, as the critic matures with experience, represent a growing stability of organisation (the problem is to combine stability with growth). What, on testing and re-testing and wider experience, turn out to be my more constant preferences, what the relative permanencies in my response, and what structure begins to assert itself in the field of poetry with which I am familiar? What map or chart of English poetry as a whole represents my utmost consistency and most inclusive coherence of response?

F. R. LEAVIS:

The Common Pursuit (Chatto and Windus, 1952)

61

*A NOVELIST'S PROBLEM**

Often, when I am writing a novel, I find myself envying the film director; he has at his disposal so many techniques for saving him trouble. Thus if he wishes to indicate a lapse of time he merely has to show a calendar with[1] its pages blowing away in the wind. And if, despite this lapse, he wishes to retain a sense of continuity, he need only repeat the final sentence in his last sequence, in a slightly different tone of voice.

Let us see what happens if, for once, we adopt this technique. We hold the camera on Bob, saying,[2] "We shall have to do something about them." Then we show the leaves blowing off our calendar—nearly a hundred of them. Then we switch back to Bob . . . but no. It will not quite work. The scene makes no sense unless we mention that during this interval of time Miss Mint fell gravely ill, and[3] it was because of her illness that things came to such a pass. Marius was away on one of his missions and I was so engaged that I did not realise what was happening. On the few occasions when I visited Miss Mint in hospital she gave no hint that anything was wrong.

It was Bob, once again, who was the indirect means of bringing things to a head, for his car, driven by the admirable and expert Alphonse, collided with the Stromens' at the bottom of the lane.

BEVERLEY NICHOLS:

Sunlight on the Lawn (Jonathan Cape, 1956)

[1] *dont.*

[2] Avoid the ambiguity of the English in translating.

[3] Repeat "that" in the French translation.

62

*MUSIC FOR FILMS****

There are two ways of writing film music. One is that in which every action, word, gesture or incident is punctuated in sound. This requires great skill and orchestral knowledge and a vivid specialised imagination, but often leads to a mere scrappy succession of sounds of no musical value in itself. On this the question arises: should film music have any value outside its particular function? By value I do not mean necessarily that it must sound equally well played as a concert piece, but I do believe that no artistic result can come from this complex entity, the film, unless each element, acting, photography, script, and music are each, in themselves and by themselves, intrinsically good.

The other method of writing film music, which personally I favour, partly because I am quite incapable of doing the first, is to ignore the details and to intensify the spirit of the whole situation by a continuous stream of music. This stream can be modified (often at rehearsal!) by points of colour superimposed on the flow. For example, your music is illustrating Columbus's voyage, and you have a sombre tune symbolising the weariness of the voyage, the depression of the crew and the doubts of Columbus. But the producer says, "I want a little bit of sunshine music for that flash on the waves." Now, don't say, "O well, the music does not provide for that; I must take it home and write something quite new." If you are wise, you will send the orchestra away for five minutes, which will delight them. Then you look at the score to find out what instruments are unemployed—say, the harp and two muted trumpets—you write in your sunlight at the appropriate second; you recall the orchestra; you then play the altered version, while the producer marvels at your skill in composing what appears to him to be an entirely new piece of music in so short a time.

R. VAUGHAN WILLIAMS:

Some Thoughts on Beethoven's Choral Symphony (Oxford University Press, 1953)

63

*THE PLOT OF "LES FAUX-MONNAYEURS"**

We have, in the first place, a plot in *Les Faux-Monnayeurs* of the logical objective type that we have been considering—a plot, or rather fragments of plots. The main fragment concerns a young man called Olivier—a charming, touching and lovable character, who misses happiness, and then recovers it after an excellently contrived *dénouement*; confers it also; this fragment has a wonderful radiance and 'lives', if I may use so coarse a word, it is a successful creation on familiar lines. But it is[1] by no means the centre of the book. No more[2] are the other logical fragments —that which concerns Georges, Olivier's schoolboy brother, who passes false coin, and is instrumental in driving a fellow-pupil to suicide. (Gide gives us his sources for all this in his diary, he got the idea of[3] Georges from a boy[4] whom he caught trying[5] to steal a book off a stall, the gang of coiners were caught at Rouen, and the suicide of children took place at Clermont-Ferrand, etc.) Neither Olivier, nor Georges, nor Vincent a third brother, nor Bernard their friend is[6] the centre of the book. We come nearer to it in Édouard. Édouard is a novelist. He bears the same relation to Gide as Clissold does[7] to Wells. I dare not be more precise. Like Gide, he keeps a diary, like Gide he is writing a book called *Les Faux-Monnayeurs*, and like Clissold he is disavowed. Édouard's diary is printed in full. It begins before the plot-fragments, continues during them, and forms the bulk of Gide's book. Édouard is not just a chronicler. He is an actor too; indeed it is he who rescues Olivier and is rescued by him; we leave those two[8] in happiness.

E. M. FORSTER:
Aspects of the Novel (Edward Arnold, 1949)

[1] § **192**. [2] Use *non plus*. See § **223**.
[3] Paraphrase to avoid ambiguity in the French.
[4] Gide uses *lycéen* in his description of this episode. [5] Use *vouloir*.
[6] For the concord with *ni . . . ni . . .* see § **310**. 2.
[7] French requires inversion here, together with a neuter pronoun. See § **343**. 5. (*c*). [8] "those two": stress in the translation. See § **324**.

64

*CÉZANNE'S WATER-COLOURS*****

Cézanne's water-colours are amongst the most perfect of his works. And, here again, one must suppose that they were unknown to those critics who have maintained that he was a clumsy or heavy-handed painter. It is true that his figure pieces are in a grave and massive style, but he was also capable of the utmost delicacy. Often these water-colours seem to be almost Whistlerian in their elegance, but Cézanne's touches of colour were applied on a very different principle. Their decorative effect is, so to say, a by-product. Their intention is to record for his own satisfaction the nodal points in a composition, and by nodal points I mean those places where the junction of the planes is of the greatest importance. The direction of these planes he represents by touches of pure colour, pale blue, pink, sienna and green, and his knowledge of their effect on one another is so sure that a very few of such transparent touches are sufficient to create an effect of great solidity.

It is in his drawings and water-colours that one recognises most clearly Cézanne's faculty of seeing both in depth and pattern at the same time. Sometimes the point he selects for notation is a piece of the background, sometimes an internal plane, yet all are related in space and subservient to a design. Out of a very complex subject he is able to select a few beautiful shapes and set them down with such certainty that we are not conscious of the white paper in between them, but only of their harmonious relation to each other.

Yet this is also the period in which Cézanne's wish to discover order in appearances becomes less insistent. His freer technique led to a more spontaneous-looking expression of his sensations, so that often the structure of a picture is almost entirely concealed. And in the 1890s, there reappears in his painting the element of romanticism which was his point of departure, and which the long period of classic constructions had seemed almost to destroy. Such a picture as the *Bridge* in Moscow, although it retains the rich texture and firm construction of the eighties, shows a re-emergence of drama. After twenty years of restraint this extremely passionate man feels sure enough of himself to speak out.

KENNETH CLARK:

Landscape into Art (John Murray, 1949)

65

*FROM AN EIGHTEENTH-CENTURY LETTER**

On this fine first of December, under an uncloudy sky, and in a room full of sunshine, I address myself to the payment of a debt long in arrear, but never forgotten by me, however I may have seemed to forget it. I will not waste time in apologies.[1] I have but one, and that one will suggest itself unmentioned.[2] I will only add that you are the first[3] to whom I write of several to whom I have[4] not written for many months, who all have claims upon me, and who I flatter myself are all grumbling at my silence. In your case perhaps I have been less anxious than in the case of some others, because if you have not heard from myself, you have heard from Mrs Unwin. From her[5] you have learned that I live, that I am as well as usual, and that I translate Homer, —— three short items, but in which is comprised the whole detail of my present history. Thus I fared when you were here; thus I have fared ever since you were here; and thus, if it please God, I shall continue to fare for some time longer; for, though the work is done, it is not finished, —— a[6] riddle which you, who are a brother of the press, will solve easily. I have also been the less anxious because I have had frequent opportunities to hear of you, and have always heard that you are in good health and happy. Of Mrs Newton, too, I have heard more favourable accounts of late, which have given us both the sincerest pleasure.

WILLIAM COWPER:

Letter to the Revd. John Newton, 1st December, 1789

[1] Translate: "in making apologies."

[2] *i.e.*, "without my mentioning it."

[3] § **196**. 4., § **325**. 2.

[4] Tense? See example with *depuis*, § **262**.

[5] § **325**. 2.

[6] § **170**. 4.

66

*WHAT IS ARCHITECTURE?***

A bicycle shed is a building; Lincoln Cathedral is a piece of architecture. Nearly everything that encloses space on a scale[1] sufficient for a human being to move in, is a building; the term architecture applies only to buildings designed with a view to aesthetic appeal. Now aesthetic sensations may be caused by a building in three different ways. First, they may be produced by the treatment of walls, proportions of windows, the relation of wall-space to window-space, of one storey to another, of ornamentation such as the tracery of a 14th-century window, or the leaf and fruit garlands of a Wren porch.[2] Secondly, the treatment of the exterior of a building as a whole is aesthetically significant, its contrasts of block against block, the effect of a pitched or flat roof or a dome, the rhythm of projections and recessions. Thirdly, there is the effect on our senses of the treatment of the interior, the sequence of rooms, the widening out of a nave at the crossing, the stately movement of a baroque staircase. The first of these three ways is two-dimensional; it is the painter's way. The second is three-dimensional; and as it treats the building as volume, as a plastic unit, it is the sculptor's way. The third is three-dimensional too, but it concerns space; it is the architect's own way more than the others. What distinguishes architecture from painting and sculpture is its spatial quality. In this, and only in this, no other artist can emulate the architect. Thus the history of architecture is primarily a history of man shaping space, and the historian must keep spatial[3] problems always in the foreground. This is[4] why no book on architecture, however popular its presentation may be, can be successful without ground-plans.

NIKOLAUS PEVSNER:

An Outline of European Architecture (John Murray, 1948)

[1] "on a scale" can be omitted in the French.
[2] "a Wren porch"—*i.e.*, "designed by Wren."
[3] "spatial." Say, "of a spatial order."
[4] § 192.

67

*WAGNER'S CONTRIBUTION TO MUSIC*****

Music could no more stop at Wagner than it could stop at Bach, Gluck, or Beethoven. The expansion of manner which music underwent at the hands of each of these men, be it noted, was the fruit of a correlative expansion of the mental world of the musician—not the individual musician, but the type. The great interest of Wagner for many of us is that with him, for the first time, music aimed at becoming co-extensive with human life. (So much, I think, may be broadly postulated without entering on very contentious grounds, if we complete the proposition by saying that Berlioz and Liszt—the Liszt of the twelve symphonic poems, the *Dante* symphony and the *Faust* symphony—are to be understood as subsumed under Wagner.) But the very element in his work that made Wagner an unquestionable evolution from Beethoven—the clear perception that in the symphony pure and simple you could never, do what you would, advance entirely out of the decorative into the human, that to concern herself more pointedly with man and the world, music must call in the aid of poetry, with its wider and deeper associations with human life—this was at the same time, curiously enough, the element that marked the limits of the opera and foretold its ultimate passing away. Opera, it is now evident, is *not* the form of either the present or the future. It was once the revolutionary form and under its red banner men imbrued their hands with the gore of their fellow-men; now it is a classic, and in twenty years we shall have a school that quotes its Wagner against the new troublers of our musical conventions as a former school quoted Mozart and Beethoven against Wagner. And why is the opera now beginning to be recognised as a limited form, instead of the universal form which Wagner fondly hoped to make it? Simply because it has now become clear to us that the admixture of the human voice in music really limits the range of the art as much as the absence of it formerly limited the symphony. What the old music needed was fertilisation by speech, as Wagner never wearied of telling us; what music at present needs is emancipation from the tyranny of speech. A glance at the aesthetic of the art will make this seem less paradoxical than it sounds at first.

ERNEST NEWMAN:
Musical Studies (John Lane, 1905)

68

*REFLECTIONS ON POETRY****

I want to continue talking about Sandburg, a reperusal of whose writings has put me in an argumentative mood. Sandburg has defined poetry as 'a series of explanations of life, fading off into horizons too swift for explanations.' In other words he is mainly concerned with the momentariness of life and his perceptions of its sensuous effect on him. Such poetry is, undisguisedly, improvisation; its spontaneity is largely conditional on not pausing to consider coherency. Selection has to be experimental and instinctive. The writer is attempting to intercept life while it is in motion. Hence the rejection of metrical stability, and the consequent sacrifice of incisiveness and intensity. An objection to this loose impressionism is that it resembles the provisional scenario or preliminary ingredients of expression rather than the finished work of art. Poetry is the result of a process, partly subconscious. Superficial demonstrations of what the poetic impulse feels like are unsatisfactory; it is doubtful whether durability can be imposed on the transitory and the evanescent. Vitally evocative poetry is the essence of innumerable apprehensions of experience. But one must admit that, in the long run, those apprehensions don't provide much to write home about. My own belief is that none of us have many things to say which are inherently memorable. Those few things are a condensation of our simplified humanity, and most of them can be traced back to childhood. They belong to what a living poet has called 'the mighty motherhood of sense', and should be used with economy and discretion. Meanwhile I mistrust random improvisings, even when performed by the pioneering genius and bright vocabulary of a Sandburg.

SIEGFRIED SASSOON:

Siegfried's Journey (Faber and Faber, 1945)

69

*PREFATORY REMARKS ON POETRY AND CRITICISM*****

In these lectures I have to deal as much or more with criticism of poetry as with poetry itself; and my subject is not merely the relation of criticism to poetry, if by that we assume that we know already what poetry is, and does, and is for. Indeed, a good part of criticism has consisted simply in the pursuit of answers to these questions. Let me start with the supposition that we do not know what poetry is, or what it does or ought to do, or of what use it is; and try to find out, in examining the relation of poetry and criticism, what the use of both of them is. We may even discover that we have no very clear idea of what *use* is; at any rate we had better not assume that we know.

I shall not begin with any general definition of what is and what is not poetry, or any discussion of whether poetry need be always in verse, or any consideration of the difference between the poetry-verse antithesis and the poetry-prose antithesis. Criticism, however, may be separated from the beginning not into two kinds, but according to two tendencies. I assume that criticism is that department of thought which either seeks to find out what poetry is, what its use is, what desires it satisfies, why it is written and why read, or recited; or which, making some conscious or unconscious assumption that we do know these things, assesses actual poetry. We may find that good criticism has other designs than these; but these are the ones which it is allowed to profess. Criticism, of course, never does find out what poetry is in the sense of arriving at an adequate definition; but I do not know of what use such a definition would be if it were found. Nor can criticism ever arrive at any final appraisal of poetry. But there are these two theoretical limits of criticism: at one of which we attempt to answer the question "what is poetry?" and at the other "is this a good poem?" No theoretic ingenuity will suffice to answer the second question, because no theory can amount to much which is not founded upon a direct experience of good poetry; but on the other hand our direct experience of poetry involves a good deal of generalising activity.

T. S. ELIOT:

The Use of Poetry (Faber and Faber, 1933)

70

*THE STRONG MAN IN FICTION***

An adventurous romance without a strong man, a hero of Herculean grit, may be entrancing, even exciting, but it is not ideal. The psychological novel, the satire, the short story, the novel of manners, these may traffic in anaemia as they will; but the perfect romance must have muscle, must tell of at least one man of might; or, as Dumas in his handsome way used to have it, of iron: D'Artagnan is 'this man of iron,' Chicot, the superb Chicot, has 'a wrist of steel.' One might go farther and say that no story with a credible strong man in it[1] can be altogether a failure. A paltry mind cannot invent a strong man. Even the strong man of the Penny Dreadful, machine-made and impossible though he be, predicates right instincts in his inventor. It is perhaps too much to say that one wants to read the story; but had one the power of life and death, one would be lenient with the muscular school.

To be[2] strong is not sufficient; and merely to fight is not sufficient. Our hero must fight against odds, the more the merrier. We ask only that[3] the fight is intelligible, reasonable, easily followed on paper, and the odds may be as heavy as the author cares to make them. Whether the last chapter should or should not describe the ultimate failure of the hero is a matter of taste. Personally, provided[4] he is not his own historian, I prefer him to live on in hard-earned peace. Of course if the story is written in the first person singular, by the hero himself, he always, or almost always, does so live on; which is an argument against that method; for in the first place the reader is robbed of surprises, and in the second his opinion of the strong man is lowered on learning that he took to the pen. The pen is so inferior a weapon. It may be mightier than the sword, but the sword is better fun.

E. V. Lucas:

"On Fighting Against Odds" from *Visibility Good* (Methuen, 1931)

[1] Use a relative phrase, such as "in which figures," "which presents," etc. [2] § **110**. [3] § **373**. [4] § **388**.

71

CALDARA'S CRUCIFIXUS****

Nevertheless, despite the great beauty of his melody and the power and individuality of his harmony, it is probably his ability to reconcile the claims of both these elements with the exigencies of an intricate and finely-wrought polyphonic texture that constitutes Caldara's chief title to lasting fame. In this respect his *Crucifixus* in sixteen real parts is one of the most remarkable works ever written. For it is not as if, like practically all other contrapuntal feats in a large number of parts, it was a mere exhibition of barren mathematical ingenuity, consisting almost entirely of a perpetual oscillation between tonic and dominant harmonies, and entirely devoid of musical interest of any kind. On the contrary, it is a work of intrinsic beauty, all technical considerations apart, and it is difficult to say which to admire the most; the beauty and expressiveness of the themes, the superb harmonic structure, or the consummate ease and mastery with which he handles such a vast number of voices. It is only at the cadences (where it is obviously unavoidable) that any strain or artificiality in the movement of the individual parts makes itself felt; otherwise they progress as naturally, logically, and inevitably as if there were only four or five of them to consider. The stupendous nature of such an achievement from the technical point of view can perhaps be fully appreciated only by those who retain painful recollections of their efforts in student days to write strict scholastic counterpoint in even such a comparatively small number of parts as seven or eight. For Caldara takes no liberties with the strict style save for the employment of hidden fifths or octaves, and consecutives by contrary motion. (Two parts moving from a unison to an octave, for example, or vice versa.) The concluding bars of this superb composition are reprinted on the pages following this essay. It is given in full score, as, owing to the continual and intricate crossing of parts, its linear beauty can be properly appreciated only when thus set forth.

CECIL GRAY:

Contingencies and other Essays (Oxford University Press, 1947)

72

*REBUKE TO A READER***

——How could you, Madam, be so inattentive in reading the last chapter? I told you in it,[1] *That my mother was not a papist.* ——Papist! You told me no such thing, Sir. ——Madam I beg leave to repeat it[2] over again, that I told you as plain, at least, as words, by direct inference, could tell you such a thing. ——Then, Sir, I must have miss'd a page. ——No, Madam, —— you have not miss'd a word. ——Then I was asleep, Sir. —— My pride, Madam, cannot allow you that refuge. ——Then, I declare, I know nothing at all about the matter. ——That, Madam, is the very fault I lay to your charge; and as a punishment for it, I do insist upon it, that you immediately turn back, that is, as soon as[3] you get to the next full stop, and read[4] the whole chapter over again. I have imposed this penance upon the lady, neither out of[5] wantonness nor cruelty; but from the best of motives; and therefore shall make her no apology for it when she returns back: ——'Tis to rebuke a vicious taste, which has crept into thousands besides herself, ——of reading straight forwards, more in quest of the adventures, than of the deep erudition and knowledge which a book of this cast, if read over as it should be, would infallibly impart with them—— The mind should be accustomed to make wise reflections, and draw curious conclusions as it goes along; the habitude of which made *Pliny* the younger affirm, "That he never read a book so bad, but he drew some profit from it."

LAURENCE STERNE:
Tristram Shandy

[1] "in it": § **229**. [2] § **223**. 2. [3] § **83**. 2.
[4] Translate: "and that you read." [5] § **286**. 2.

73

*A KING OF JAZZ****

Fats Waller was unique, and for this reason it will be useless to try and trace any future development of his style. It can be copied, of course, with varying success, but the imitation is usually so poor a carbon copy that it is pointless.

His uniqueness lies in the fact that he achieved world fame in both the popular sense of the word and in the jazz field, an extremely difficult feat, for in most cases excursions into the realm of 'what the public likes' result in an adulteration of artistic integrity. An artist may produce drivel for public consumption and create things that really matter for his own benefit, or for the benefit of a few friends to appreciate.[1] The drivel he may serve up with his tongue in his cheek, carefully turned away from his audience.

Fats Waller managed to take some of the rubbish which he knew the public enjoyed, and, by his own legerdemain, transmuted it into an enjoyable guying of its own worst aspects. Not only that, he managed to take the public into his confidence, as if he were saying: "Now look, you know this is tripe, and I know it's tripe, but let's see what we can do with it to make it palatable, and, at the same time, see if we can have some jazz and get a little fun out of it."

This must not be taken to imply that he was always the lovably satirical entertainer. His piano solos, and his work as a rhythm section pianist with many jazz groups, point to a jazz feeling and interpretation which is unequalled in many respects, and that inborn sense led him to make the classic reply to a lady who asked him what rhythm was. He replied simply and in perfect good faith: "Lady, if you has to ask, you ain't got it."

He has no history of knocking around the dives of New Orleans or Chicago, listening with bated breath to the legendary jazz 'greats,' no marching in the second line of a street parade, for he was born in Harlem and his father, Pastor Waller, intended him to follow in his footsteps, perhaps in time to preach at the Abyssinian Baptist Chapel. To prepare him for this, he was given piano and organ lessons, and, as a boy, used to play the harmonium at open-air prayer meetings.

REX HARRIS:

Jazz (Penguin, 1952)

[1] Avoid the tautology of the English.

74

*THE SHAKESPEARE WONDER*****

What a fine confusion must Shakespeare's life have been! By the Thames he was wresting beauty from a bear-garden, competing with a raree-show of bull-baiting and blood-boltered carnival amid a welter of lusty living, loving, and carousing. By the Avon he was carefully investing what he won in London. To look for the essential Shakespeare is immediately to be confronted with the major and ever-engrossing Elizabethan mystery. The question is, concisely, this. How could an epoch so brutish and so cruel in its pursuit of power and pleasure have been so delicate in its pursuit of the tender passion, the verbal beauty, and the musical harmonies which were always so ravishing to Shakespeare's sensibility?

How close can we come to that London of 1600 which was at once scaffold, whipping-post, baiting-ring, music-box for 'heavenly harmony,' and platform of the sons of Apollo? Often there have been these associations, these queer cousins among human doings and desires, but scarcely ever were they packed so close together as in Elizabeth's tiny London and especially on the Southwark shore of the busy, music-ringing Thames.

It is an undrained, unwatered, fetid London, with plague ever waiting to pounce, its scavengers the rats and kites and carrion-crows. Yet the wits who are being rowed over from the Inns of Court are dressed in the exquisite foppery of the world. Their talk is carved into conceits. They have lutes and voices and they sing lyrics as fine-spun in beauty as any ever wrought by this most lyrical of nations. Done with their voyage and their madrigals, they join the stench and squalor of the Paris Garden mob and enter the Globe to hear the mightiest of lines, the tenderest of songs, the dying fall of an iambic on some boy-player's lips, word-music which went whispering out of Southwark into the airstream of the ages and is now for ever on the lips of men. Two lines of a Shakespeare sonnet sum up the paradox of the City and the time in which the man was working,

> How 'gainst this rage shall beauty hold a plea
> Whose action is no stronger than a flower?

Life raged, coarse as a hurricane, about the roots of English poetry then: but the flower held.

That is one reason why this Shakespeare Wonder appeals especially to me. To seek to probe this paradox of beastliness and beauty is adventure enough. Curiosity, steeled by a combative loyalty, is the spur. Combative, because every man fights for his own Shakespeare: loyal, because without devotion nobody would take the trouble to retread so much hard-trodden ground. What William Shakespeare wrote (in all sincerity, I think) to Henry Wriothesley, Earl of Southampton, in the preface to *Lucrece*, I make bold to apply to him, who is my subject, "What I have done is yours; what I have to do is yours: being part in all I have, devoted yours." In short, this is a lover's book.

IVOR BROWN:
Shakespeare (Collins, 1949)

75

*PROBLEMS OF SUCCESSFUL WRITING***

If you write a novel, it is possible that you may find a publisher willing to put it on the market at his own risk. At the worst he would be jeopardising some three or four hundred pounds. He may suggest one or two changes to you, but in the main they will be artistic changes, designed to improve your novel as a novel.

Should you, however, write a play, which is going to cost three or four thousand pounds to put on in the West End, you will find the manager far more cautious than the publisher. He will show a greater disposition to tinker with your play, and, for scenes which are perhaps original and therefore, in his mind, risky, to substitute episodes of a type which have frequently been known to succeed in the theatre, and are therefore reckoned safe. In other words, he does not wish to invest his money without making as sure as he knows how that he will get it back, plus a reasonable profit. You will be lucky indeed if your play is heard on the first night without alterations which seem to you substantial, and—to say the least—artistically undesirable.

But if[1] the form which your self-expression has taken should be a screen play, which may well cost a hundred thousand pounds or a hundred and fifty thousand to put before the public, then you will find the people who put down the money exceedingly cautious. They will show an acute disposition to meddle with your story, and, for the scenes on which you have set your heart, to substitute others of a hackneyed kind for which the public has already shown a liking. You will be requested to alter various characters to suit the personalities of the stars whom the studio has engaged as one means of ensuring that their investment will not go down the drain.

The stars are necessary, or are[2] thought to be necessary by the business men involved in films, because the public go to see this or that star rather than this or that story. Put two popular stars opposite each other in practically any story you like, and their fans will attend the cinemas.

L. A. G. STRONG:
The Writer's Trade (Methuen, 1953)

[1] "But if." Say, "But if your self-expression should take," etc. Tense of "should take"? See § **85**.

[2] "are thought": use the active voice.

76

*THE EUROPEAN CONVENTION IN PAINTING****

It is appropriate at this point to make a short but important digression into the realms of style, and to remember that the whole weight of European tradition has been built up, since the beginning of the Renaissance, on the assumption that the painter must cover the whole surface of his picture with descriptive matter. I am not referring to the theory of realism, but to the more fundamental theory that the whole of his picture must have a descriptive *meaning*.[1] This theory has bitten so deep into the consciousness of every European that we have ceased to think of it as extraordinary or even interesting. We have ceased to realise it at all. And yet it has by no means always been accepted by other civilisations. An area of blue paint in the upper part of a landscape by Constable *means* a cloudless sky. An area of green paint in the background of a still life by Picasso *means* a green wall. However distorted the forms in the picture may be, the very fact that one can use the word 'background' shows that one sees the picture as a representation of objects in space, and that Picasso, though he has outgrown the Renaissance view of life, has not, for all his revolutionary courage, abandoned the Renaissance theory of painting.

One has only to remember that a plain sky in a Chinese landscape is *not* intended to indicate an absence of clouds but only a refusal to make any statement about clouds, and that the area of silk or paper 'behind' a Chinese still life is *not* in any sense a representation of a featureless background, in order to realise that the Renaissance theory that every square inch of a painting must convey visual information is certainly not a universally accepted theory. The European picture, however stylised or distorted, is always basically a representation: the Chinese picture is a self-contained symbol. The same is true of mediaeval European art. Visual information, even about forms that exist only in the artist's imagination, is not part of its intention. Renaissance art has no alternative but to accept that intention; and the average adult European to-day is forced, by the tradition in which he grew up, to make the same set of assumptions when he looks at a painting.

ERIC NEWTON:

The Meaning of Beauty (Longmans, Green, 1950)

[1] Where possible bring out the force of the italicized words by means other than italics.

77

*ART AND THE PUBLIC***

Less and less[1]—with the development of democracy, the spread of education, the increase of opportunity, through travelling exhibitions and multiplied reproductions, to become familiar with works of art—can the normal consumer be ignored. The curious situation[2] in which art becomes more and more available to the average man—whose experience is most complete on the outer, the less abstract levels of painting, while the artist himself is concentrating more and more on the inner, the more purely aesthetic levels—must be faced. For in the process of facing it, the meaning of the word 'beauty' will surely emerge. At present the word becomes more difficult to use every day, yet the basic hunger for it persists, and even grows, as the opportunity for experiencing it grows.

The easiest way to face it will be to examine the normal *conservative* attitude to contemporary art, the attitude of the man who, accepting the Albertian theory of art ('truth plus beauty' as he would put it), is puzzled and distressed to find that a great many contemporary works of art seem to him both untrue and ugly, and that those very works of art are consistently praised by a small but far from negligible body of critics and art-lovers.

ERIC NEWTON:

The Meaning of Beauty (Longmans, Green, 1950)

[1] It would be more natural, in French, to leave the conclusion until the end of the sentence, and not wrap it about the evidence, as in the English. Say, for example, "With the development . . . it becomes more and more difficult," etc.

[2] The syntax of this sentence again needs to be modified for translation purposes.

78

*SELECTION AND EMPHASIS*****

We live in an everlasting battle, an everlasting creation which produces the endless revolution of politics and ideas that perplexes the morning paper. Of course, the turmoil of actual events is deeper than that. It is a true chaos; it includes an immense element of luck, of pure chance. For, although all events are determined, those that are ideas for action formed in some mind are partly self-determined and unpredictable. This brings uncertainty into every chain of causation where one link is the human will. What's more, so far as we are concerned as people, although all events belong to chains of causation, the chains are not synchronised. The individual going for a walk could not ascertain the chain of causes that sent a careful driver with a good car, an errand boy on a bicycle and a summer shower to combine in producing the skid that is going to kill him.

That is why a world of reality that possesses such definite forms both of fact and feeling, presents itself to us as chaos, a place full of nonsense, of injustice, of bad luck; and why children spend so much of their time asking questions. They are trying to build up, each for himself, some comprehensible idea by which to guide their conduct in such a terrifying confusion.

They find the task extremely difficult. Often they get the wrong answers to their questions, and also they easily get the answers wrong. For words need interpretation and the interpretation depends very much, not only on the selection of the words, but the emphasis given to the words, on the quality of the words and on the tone of voice with which they are spoken. It is the selection, the emphasis, the tone, that gives the valuation. If a child is told, "Don't eat too much cake," and "Don't torture the cat," with the same mild emphasis, it will regard both actions with the same indulgence.

This selection, this tone, this emphasis is art. Almost all use of language is art, and particularly all communication between us, all communication that not only gives the facts, but also puts some valuation on the facts, is art. There is no other means by which the feeling about a fact can be conveyed.

JOYCE CARY:

Art and Reality (Cambridge University Press, 1958)

79

*THE DEVELOPMENT OF HUMAN CONSCIOUSNESS***

If I may use an image myself, human consciousness has been represented in this argument as an octopus of unimaginable dimensions with tentacles ever weaving through the surrounding elements, searching and advancing everywhere, twitching and withdrawing when danger is sensed, but gradually mastering its environment, gradually increasing the range of its knowledge and activity. At the end of each tentacle is the sensitive, image-forming perception of the artist. To complete the image, one must think of[1] our monster as proceeding in a definite direction, towards some goal not fully realised, animated by some instinct for a fuller and securer life.

This creature has now moved into a new habitat—no longer a habitat of horses and carriages and Newtonian cosmology, no longer a habitat of dark cavelike houses and aristocratic patronage—but a world of electric energy and relativity, of glass and steel, of speed and democratic uniformity. The artist has helped to create this brave new world—with his images. He now moves on towards another and still braver world, and he has the present task of creating images that will adumbrate this world, make it imaginatively conceivable to the alert mentality of modern man. How shall he do this? With images of the past—the Greek image of ideal man, the Gothic image of a transcendental God, the Renaissance image of a serene Arcadia? None of these images has any longer any relevance. The artist must now create new images, images of a possible new world, a world possible in this era of scientific transformation. And this is[2] what the constructive artist is trying to do. "He has found the means and the methods," as Gabo says, "to create new images and to convey them as emotional manifestations in our everyday experience."

Sir Herbert Read:

Icon and Idea (Faber and Faber, 1955)

[1] "think of . . . as." Say, "imagine that." [2] § **192**.

80

*TWO TYPES OF VISION IN PAINTING****

The change from linear vision and emphasis upon outlines which appeared to limit and define objects came in the sixteenth century and, historically, it was associated with the Italian painters of the Catholic Reaction. Instead of the natural world being regarded as a congeries of tangible masses and objects, the characteristics of the immensity of space and continual movement, which experience also finds in Nature, were recognised, and simultaneously the craft methods of painters altered in order that these characteristics might find expression. The linear method had given the world the beauty of a Raphael masterpiece. The less defined and more fluid treatment in a great Rubens was to reveal something which the modern outlook regards as no less beautiful and, assuredly, more significant.

At the risk of repetition, it will be worth while emphasising the distinction between the two types of vision. In linear vision, the eye searches for and follows what seems to be the outlines of things. Not so, in what may be called 'painterly' vision.

Now patches of light, of shade and of colour impress themselves vividly upon the mind and call for expression. Looking at a turning wheel, what seems important is not the wheel, but the turning. The spokes may be disregarded, and yet, strangely enough, the fact that they are no longer represented as separate spokes gives the very impression of movement which the painter is seeking.

ERNEST SHORT:

A History of British Painting (Eyre and Spottiswoode, 1953)

81

*ART IN THE INDUSTRIAL AGE*****

The herding of a rapidly-increasing population into the enormous, hideous barrack-like towns of the industrial regions destroyed irreparably the older ways of life, substituting for the varied nourishment of the soil the meagre, processed diet of hard facts which Mr Gradgrind prescribed for the inhabitants of Coketown. At the same time as the emotional life of the masses was being steadily impoverished, their response to the imaginative use of words becoming ever more sluggish, the resources of language at the disposal of the more sophisticated poets grew richer and more elaborate than ever before, thanks to the scores of new words invented during the nineteenth century and to the hitherto uncharted modes of expression which were explored by the first Romantics and their followers. At the end of the nineteenth century there stretched an enormous gulf between the greasy, threadbare speech of the lower-middle classes and the highly specialised, self-conscious language of poetry, a gulf which has widened during the present century. For, in the past fifty years, a multitude of professional entertainers, journalists, advertisers, song-writers, script-writers, scenario-writers, and other peddlers of anodynes have made their living by providing millions of people with the emotional sustenance which they can no longer find for themselves. They have discovered that the easiest way to satisfy their clients is to arouse their passions and play on their feelings by exploiting the most obvious associations of words which the imperfectly educated regard as romantic and beautiful, thereby exemplifying the melancholy truth of W. B. Yeats's adage: "Every country likes good art till it produces its own form of vulgarity and after that will have nothing else."

JOHN PRESS:

The Chequer'd Shade (Oxford University Press, 1958)

82

*THE HAND OF GLORY****

On one of the bleakest and bravest English roads I know, the Roman road which breasts the Pennines at Scotch Corner and soars over the noble waste of Stainmore to Brough and Carlisle, there is a lonely steading called the Hand of Glory. This glittering name for a moorland house of call refers back to a macabre crime. It is a title that stays in the mind and to me it has long seemed the apt, the final phrase for[1] the fingers that can be seen in effigy stiffly clutching a quill below the unworthy bust in Stratford Church. There never was such a hand for the use of words, and such a hand, maybe, there never again will be. Nothing in our literature, nothing, perhaps, in any literature, has such a quality of supremacy, nothing is so unchallengeable, as Shakespeare's power, through that Hand of Glory, to put observation and feeling into words.

It is this very sovereignty of Shakespeare's that has made some deny him the crown. If he had been only a little ahead of the others, would there have been so much effort to prove that 'Shagsper' of petty Stratford could not have been the man? But he was so easily the best that people have found it difficult to believe that he was real. Chesterton said of Dickens that he was not a man but a mob; Shakespeare, in his use of words, was not a man but a miracle. And where you get miracles, you are bound to get doubt and denial. Nobody can say that the lines were never written; but they can and do deny that they were written by the Warwickshire lad turned strolling player. The sceptics stress the ignorance of Stratford, on which they have been sufficiently refuted. There were plenty of books and readers in the town; moreover, Shakespeare does not make the country folk in his plays illiterate. The shepherds provide a market for printed ballads as well as for baubles. Young Richard Quiney of Stratford wrote to his father Adrian in flowing and correct Latin at the age of eleven. To say that Shakespeare could not have picked up a good Ovidian Latinity at Stratford is nonsense.

IVOR BROWN:

Shakespeare (Collins, 1949)

[1] Use a phrase to translate "for."

83

*CONCRETE IN ARCHITECTURE*****

To a considerable extent Perret had succeeded in achieving what he had long consciously sought, that is, a vocabulary of design in concrete as direct, as expressive, and as ordered as the masonry vocabulary of the seventeenth and eighteenth centuries—a *style Louis XX*, so to say—still very French in a quite traditional way, yet unmistakably of this century. In the Garde Meuble or National Furniture Storehouse in the Rue Croulebarbe in Paris, begun the next year, the vocabulary is—from principle—all but identical; yet fewer windows and more solid panels were necessary here so that the general effect is flatter and blanker. The curved colonnade across the open side of the court is almost archaeologically reminiscent of the eighteenth century, despite the breadth of its spans and the ingenuity of its detailing. The small concert hall of 1929 in the Rue Cardinet for the École Normale de Musique is less pretentious but also less impressive.

Concrete to Perret, after all these years of employing it, was not a crude or a substitute material. By the use of coloured aggregates which he found various means of exposing he was able to vary the texture and colour of his poured and pre-cast elements with considerable subtlety and elegance. In the later buildings the workmanship is usually of the highest quality—it was by no means so in the early twenties—with arrises brought to a sharp edge in pure cement and such classicising details as the flute-like facets on piers and the capital-like treatment of their tops carried to a finish comparable to that of chisel-cut freestone.

Thus Perret was eventually able to avoid the industrial brutality of much work in concrete where the material is left as it comes from rough timber forms with crumbling arrises and pockmarked surfaces. Such lack of finish is acceptable in large-scale engineering work but certainly awkward when seen close to as in Notre-Dame at Le Raincy. On the other hand, Perret kept well away also from that slickness of surface—especially popular with younger architects in the twenties—that is produced when concrete is covered with a smooth stucco rendering and painted.

H. R. HITCHCOCK:
Architecture: 19th and 20th Centuries (Penguin, 1958)

84

*THE SPOKEN WORD***

I come back to this, then—that it is[1] the essence of the spoken word to suggest rather than to state. And this is[2] something which not only the act of hearing requires, but also the situation of the speaker. When we write, we must do what we can for our meaning while we write. For once we have printed it or posted it, we have sent it out to where it must stand on its own legs. If it succeeds by itself in expressing to the reader what we intended it to express, we shall have written it well. But how utterly different is our situation when we speak! We are then never at any moment having to set something or establish something where we must leave it. The essence of speaking is that we are not normally alone, we are face to face with someone and can continue to improvise and add to what we have said for as long as our hearer will listen to us. What we are after is only to start in his mind some ferment of thought or imagination.

What we must do at all costs, if we are to speak successfully, is to provoke him to some[3] response. If our listener responds by talking himself, we shall submit ourselves contentedly in turn to his influence. But if his response is silent, we shall be equally content to adapt what we say next to what we guess is[4] the direction of his thought, correcting and adding to his impressions as we choose. But,[5] verbal or silent, some response is always what we speak for. The jump we want is back to ourselves and not to independent conclusions. We speak to keep our man, to establish between us all sorts of relations. Our speech must be as quick as our sympathy, as flexible as our personalities. For the words we speak are to be bridges we swarm across, and the entrances we shall gain over them are, barring physical contact and whatever carpet the eye can lay, the most personal and rewarding access we can have to each other.

CHRISTOPHER SALMON:
"Broadcasting, Speech and Writing" from *The Mint* (Routledge, 1946)

[1] More simply: "the essence is . . . to," etc.

[2] § **192**. [3] § **252**. [4] "is." Translate: "to be."

[5] Recast for translation purposes, *e.g.*, "But we always speak in order to produce," etc.

85

*THE POETIC QUALITY OF JEAN DE MEUN****

This passage represents Jean's highest reach as a poet. No one who remembers the fatuity of most poetical attempts to describe heaven—the dull catalogues of jewellery and mass-singing—will underrate this green park, with its unearthly peace, its endless sunshine and fresh grass and grazing flocks. It represents also what may be called his point of maximum differentiation: in this passage he is most *unlike* Chaucer, or Guillaume de Lorris, or (for the matter of that) Dante. Does it also represent his final view of love? The answer, I think, is that Jean de Meun has no final view either of love or of anything else. This is but another aspect of his formlessness. The same defect which prevented him from writing a poem (as opposed to a mere heap of poetry) prevented him also from combining his ideas into any consistent whole. His work reads best in quotation because his mind—if I may hazard the metaphor—reads best in quotation. On any subject presented to him—and his reading presented him with nearly every subject—he can think vigorously: and from his thought his imagination catches fire: and he has language at will to make poetry of that result. But it is always a short flight. To-morrow he will be thinking differently, feeling differently, making a different kind of poetry. He lacks the power, or the will, to unify these inspired moments. Thus he tackles the problem of courtly love in several different ways, and tackles it in all of them with considerable success. In one place he is all for ridicule; and the ridicule (though it contains none of his best work) is lively enough. In another place he follows the school of Chartres; and his naturalism about sex produces noble verses. In a third place he will be a mystic; and on this theme of human and divine love he keeps a respectable place, despite the greatness of those who here become his rivals. But while all these solutions are good, the fatal defect is that they really have nothing to do with one another.

C. S. Lewis:

The Allegory of Love (Oxford University Press, 1936)

86

*A MODERN PAINTING TECHNIQUE*****

But at some point in 1944 de Staël discovered that he could dispense with line and he began composing with fat little squares or oblongs of thick, brushed paint. The grave, complex, strong works of 1945–48 were the result—and not unlike the work of the brothers van Velde of the same time. But it must have been sometime in 1949 or 1950 that he evolved that massive, squarish blob which was henceforth to dominate his entire art and which is seen, endlessly repeated (large and small, neater or more ragged, squarer or more oblong) throughout the lower half of that magnificent masterpiece, "Les Toits, 1952," reproduced on this page.

This squarish blob is de Staël's archetype of form. With this device of a mound of thick and gritty pigment forced down on to the canvas with the blade of that sort of wedge-shaped 'scraper' knife which decorators use for getting old wallpaper off walls, de Staël discovered a new means for creating spatial planes. And this discovery has echoed more widely in the work of contemporary painters, both in Europe and America, than any other post-war pictorial innovation. The immense plastic power of these round-cornered squares of flat, matt, cement-like paint is not easy to account for. Perhaps it lies in their *floating* freedom from any scaffolding of drawing? Each dense, opaque plane floats at a different depth, away from the picture-surface: each thus registers a different spatial recession; no two planes exist at the same depth. The fact that these great lozenges, in the lower half of "Les Toits," derive from city roofs, is not supremely important. Indeed, we find it difficult to reconstruct any exact feature of the Paris rooftops. It is enough that a rectilinear, architectural metropolitan *rhythm* controls all the chunky forms which recede from the bottom of this wonderful canvas up (and away) to the line of the horizon. It is enough that we are out of doors. The atmospheric blue-greys and broken whites create the city haze.

PATRICK HERON:

"Nicolas de Staël" from *The Listener* of 3rd May, 1956

CONVERSATIONAL

87

*POIROT MISSES A VISITOR**

We arrived at the flat at about twenty to two.

George, Poirot's immaculate and extremely English manservant,[1] opened the door.

"A Dr Tanios is waiting to see you, sir. He has been here for[2] half an hour."

"Dr Tanios? Where is he?"

"In the sitting-room, sir. A lady also called to see you, sir. She seemed very distressed to find you were absent from home. It was before I received your telephone message, sir, so I could not tell her when you would be returning to London."

"Describe this lady."

"She was[3] about five-foot-seven, sir, with dark hair and light blue eyes. She was wearing a grey coat and skirt and a hat worn very much to the back of the head instead of over the right eye."

"Mrs Tanios," I ejaculated in a low voice.

"She seemed in a condition of great nervous excitement, sir. Said it was of the utmost importance she should find you quickly."

"What time was this?"

"About half past ten, sir."

Poirot shook his head as he passed on towards the sitting-room.

"That is the second time I have missed hearing what Mrs Tanios has to say. What would you say, Hastings? Is there a fate in it?"

"Third time lucky," I said consolingly.

Poirot shook his head doubtfully.

AGATHA CHRISTIE:
Dumb Witness (Collins, 1937)

[1] Translate: "George, Poirot's manservant, immaculate," etc.

[2] § **73**, 1.

[3] *être* or *avoir*?

88

*A BEREAVEMENT**

"Aunt Miranda is dead," said Adrian, and broke into tears.

"Yes, yes, I know, my boy," said Mr Pettigrew. "The news came in time to prevent my coming to you[1] yesterday. It is a sad break-up for you all."

"Things are to go on in the same way."

"But to you they cannot be the same."

"Miss Wolsey is to be here instead of Aunt Miranda."

"But to you she cannot take her place, good though her intentions will[2] doubtless be."

"I expect she will think more about us."

Mr Pettigrew looked a question.

"Cousin Rosebery thought you ought not to come until after the funeral."

"I should not have done so, unless I had received a message. But I had one from your uncle, asking me to come as usual."

"He said it was better for us to be occupied."

"And I think it is," said Mr Pettigrew, looking at his pupil. "So we will attend to his wish."

"Will Pettigrew be paid for the day he did not come?" said Adrian, in an aside.

"Come, come, the occasion is not a usual one," said Mr Pettigrew, suggesting what he accepted as this. "You seem to have a sense of it, and you should behave accordingly."

"It is that, that makes him self-conscious," said Alice.

The tutor looked at Adrian in enlightenment.

"It doesn't," said the latter. "I don't think about myself."

"Then you are an unusual person. Not that[3] I should rank myself amongst those most subject to the tendency."

I. Compton-Burnett:
Mother and Son (Gollancz, 1955)

[1] Compare this phrase with the examples given in § **237**. 1.
[2] § **253**. Should a 'future subjunctive' be used? See § **86**. 3.
[3] See § **387** (restrictive clauses).

89

*LIFE ON A SUB-TROPICAL ISLAND***

"As compared with[1] England," Keith pursued, "life here is intense, palpitating, dramatic—a kind of blood-curdling farce full of irresponsible crimes and improbable consequences. The soil is saturated with blood. People are always killing themselves or each other for motives, which to an Englishman, are altogether outside the range of comprehensibility. Shall I tell you about one of our most interesting cases? I happened to be on the island at the time. There was a young fellow here—an agreeable young fellow—an artist; he was rich; he took a villa, and painted. We all liked him. Then, by degrees, he became secretive and moody. Said he was studying mechanics. He told me himself that much as he liked landscape painting he thought an artist—a real artist, he said—ought to be versed in ancillary sciences; in fortification, wood-carving, architecture, and so on. Leonardo da Vinci, you know. Well, one day they could not get into his bedroom. They broke open his door and discovered that he had constructed a perfectly formed guillotine; the knife had fallen; his head lay on one side and his body on the other. You may well be surprised. I went carefully into that case. He was in the best of health, and with a creditable artistic record behind him. He had no troubles, financial or domestic."

"Then what on earth——?"

"The scenery of Nepenthe. It got on his nerves; it unstrung him. Does that surprise you too? Don't you feel its effect upon yourself? The bland winds, the sea shining in velvety depths as though filled with some electric fluid, the riot of vegetation, these extravagant cliffs that change colour with every hour of the day? Look at that peak yonder—is it not almost transparent, like some crystal of amethyst? This coast-line alone—the sheer effrontery of its mineral charm—might affect some natures to such an extent as to dislocate their stability. Northern minds seem to become fluid here, impressionable, unstable, unbalanced—what you please."

NORMAN DOUGLAS:
South Wind (Secker, 1917)

[1] § **158**. 1.

90

*A DISAGREEMENT OVER THE SCHOOL GAME**

JOHNSTONE. Well, now you've come, I hope you're going to take a sensible view of this matter.

DIGBY. What matter, sir?

JOHNSTONE. What matter, boy? About changing the school game, of course.

DIGBY. Oh, yes, of course, sir.

JOHNSTONE. Now I hope you're going to be sensible about it, Digby. I sent for you, so that we can discuss any outstanding difficulties before the committee meets. (*Stiffening.*) Of course, if Crescent continue to stand out, there's no point in holding the meeting.

DIGBY. Well, I'm afraid, sir——

JOHNSTONE. What?

DIGBY. That Crescent have decided *against*[1] changing.

JOHNSTONE. But this—this—is preposterous! . . . Simply preposterous!

DIGBY. But we're quite within our rights, sir!

JOHNSTONE. What rights, boy?

DIGBY. The Games Committee Rules state quite clearly that before any change can be made in the school games, all the Houses must give their consent.

JOHNSTONE. Unfortunately, that is so.

DIGBY. Unfortunately, sir?

JOHNSTONE (*heavily*). Yes, sir, *un*fortunately. When the Games Committee Rules were drawn up, no one foresaw any such impossible situation as this.

DIGBY. Don't you think, sir, that the consent of all the

Houses was made necessary, just because someone *did* foresee such a situation as this?

JOHNSTONE (*glancing at him sharply*). Don't be facetious, boy!

DIGBY. I'm sorry, sir, I didn't mean to be facetious. I'm trying to be as serious as I can, sir.

JOHNSTONE. All right, I accept that. . . . But can't you see, Digby, what an advantage it would be to the School if we played rugby?

DIGBY. Well—I'm not convinced of that, sir. It's not as if we were the *only* school playing soccer.

JOHNSTONE. Oh, yes, I know there are some left, of course. But if we played rugby, we should get a far better fixture list. As it is, we have to make up the list by playing one or two local teams . . . Workmen's teams . . . the polloi.

DIGBY. Well, don't you think, sir, in its way, that's a good thing?

JOHNSTONE (*as if unable to believe his ears*). What?

DIGBY. Don't you think it would be rather bad if rugby became the privilege of people with money, while soccer was played only by the lower classes? After all, sir, sport ought not to recognise class distinctions.

JOHNSTONE. You know, I'm trying to understand you, my boy, but you make it exceedingly difficult for one.

TRAVERS OTWAY:

The Hidden Years (Faber and Faber, 1948)

[1] Bring out the force of italicised words (apart from stage directions) by means other than italics.

91

*BURGLARS**

Mr Folyot walked into his wife's room at five o'clock in the afternoon with an evening paper which he had purchased at King's Cross. Mrs Folyot was sitting up in bed having tea and feeling what is called, in[1] patients, brighter, as[2] is usual at tea-time.

"Well, dear," she said, "have you heard our news? We had the most tiresome night of burglars; they blacked poor Raymond's eye and gagged and bound him and went off with a bag of silver. Most annoying. But they say it always happens at last to everyone. Did you enjoy your conference?"

"No. Very poor." But the little cloud which the memory of a conference not enjoyed had summoned[3] to Mr Folyot's brow was dispersed by the contents of his newspaper.

"You certainly seem to have had an odd night. Or, anyhow, it comes out well in the *Evening Wire*. Where did they get all this stuff from?"

"I'm sure I don't know. Newspapers do,[4] don't they. What do they say of it?"

Mr Folyot read it aloud, in those scholarly, cultivated accents that make the press sound so surprising.

ROSE MACAULAY:

Keeping up Appearances (Collins, 1928)

[1] § **290**. [2] *ce qui*. [3] Word order. See § **343**. 5.
[4] "do." A phrase is needed in the French to bring out the meaning of the verb substitute.

92

*A FALSE START**

Gumbril Junior shrugged his[1] shoulders. "I was bored, I decided[2] to cease being a schoolmaster." He spoke with a fine airy assumption[3] of carelessness. "How are you, Mr Porteous?"

"Thank you, invariably well."

"Well, well," said Gumbril Senior, sitting down again,[4] "I must say I'm not surprised. I'm only surprised that you stood it, not being a born pedagogue, for as long as you did.[5] What ever induced you to think of turning usher, I can't imagine." He looked at his son first through his spectacles, then over the top of them; the motives of the boy's conduct revealed themselves to neither vision.

"What else[6] was there for me to do?" asked Gumbril Junior, pulling up a chair towards the fire. "You gave me a pedagogue's education and washed your hands of me. No opportunities, no openings. I had no alternative. And now you reproach me."

Mr Gumbril made an impatient gesture. "You're talking nonsense," he said. "The only point of the kind of education you had is this, it gives a young man leisure to find out what he's interested in. You apparently weren't sufficiently interested in anything——"

"I am interested in everything," interrupted Gumbril Junior.

"Which comes to the same thing," said his father parenthetically, "as being interested in nothing." And he went on from the point at which he had been interrupted. "You weren't sufficiently interested in anything to want to devote yourself to it."

ALDOUS HUXLEY:
Antic Hay (Chatto and Windus, 1923)

[1] § **178**. 1. [2] § **112**. 1.
[3] Use a gerundive construction. See § **113**. 3.
[4] Use a French verb that dispenses with a separate adverb.
[5] § **223**. [6] *d'autre, de mieux*. Position in the sentence?

93

*FOG AT SEA**

The second blast of the siren brought little groups wandering along by the rail, some talking excitedly, some peering out into the dense bank of fog into which the vessel seemed to have slid. A young woman approached the little knot of deck-chairs and asked nervously:

"Oh, Miss Monaghan, have the engines stopped? What is it, do you think?"

"They haven't. Don't talk so much, but listen."

"Yes. I think they can be heard. Someone said we'd stopped."

"No reason why the Captain shouldn't stop if he wishes. It's his affair."

"Oh, but in this fog. There must be something wrong!"

"Not so much as there might be if he didn't[1] slow down."

"Where are we, and why has it come over foggy?"

"Fog does[2] occur on the ocean, you know. You can't dry-clean it, though I believe an American firm is willing to try."

They all laughed, but as if in the spirit of mischief the Miss Monaghan addressed went on, "We're in the neighbourhood of St Paul's Rocks."

"Is that an island?"

"No. Rocks. Quite uninhabited and waterless."

The girl shuddered. "I hope we don't run aground on them."

"I should say that's just what the Captain thinks."

"He's just gone up on to the bridge."

"There. What did I tell you?"

"I'm scared stiff."

"You needn't be. Here's Mr Bowling, all ready to put you in a boat and row to[3] England."

Once again they all laughed, but the girl's teeth were chattering, and again the siren howled like some great beast in agony, and heavy drops of moisture rattled down from the streaming awnings.

R. H. MOTTRAM:

One Hundred and Twenty-eight Witnesses (Hutchinson, 1951)

[1] Tense? [2] Bring out the force of "does" in the translation.
[3] "to": translate by a verb. "row": translate by an explanatory phrase.

94

*SIZING UP THE SITUATION***

I lunched that day with Mary—alone, for her aunts were both in Paris—and it would have been hard to find in the confines of the British islands a more dejected pair. Mary, who had always a singular placid gentleness, showed her discomposure only by her pallor. As for me I was as restless as a bantam.

"I wish I had never touched the thing," I cried. "I have done more harm than good."

"You have found Lord Mercot," she protested.

"Yes, and lost Turpin. The brutes are still three up on us. We thought we had found two, and now we have lost Miss Victor again. And Turpin! They'll find him an ugly customer, and probably take strong measures with him. They'll stick to him and the girl and the little boy now like wax; for last night's performance is bound to make them suspicious."

"I wonder," said Mary, always an optimist. "You see, Sir Archie only dragged him in because of his rank. It looked odd his being[1] in Adela's company, but then all the times he has seen her he never spoke a word to her. They must have[2] noticed that. I'm anxious about Sir Archie. He ought to leave London."

"Confound him! He's going to, as soon as he gets out of hospital, which will probably be this afternoon. I insisted on it but he meant to in any case. He's heard an authentic report of a green sandpiper nesting somewhere. It would be a good thing if Archie would stick to birds. He has no head for anything else. . . . And now we've got to start again at the beginning."

"Not quite the beginning," she interposed.

"Dashed near it. They won't bring Miss Victor into that kind of world again, and all your work goes for nothing, my dear. It's uncommon bad luck[3] that you didn't begin to wake her up, for then she might have done something on her own account. But she's still a dummy, and tucked away, you may be sure, in some place where we can never reach her. And we have little more than three weeks left."

John Buchan:

The Three Hostages (Hodder and Stoughton, 1924)

[1] Could be simplified for translation purposes: "It was odd to see him," etc. [2] § **94**. 2. [3] § **379**.

95

*AN URGENT SUMMONS**

The telephone bell rang. It was a trunk call, and among the murmurs, clangings, and whispers of the operation, I had the meaningless apprehension that sometimes catches hold[1] as one listens and waits.

Then I heard Roy's voice:

"Is that you, Lewis?"

The words were precise and clear, isolated in sound.

"Yes."

"You should come down[2] to-night. There's a train in half an hour. It would be good if you caught that."

"What's the matter?"

"You should come at once. Morcom and I are certain you should come at once. Can you?"

"Can't you tell me? Is it necessary?"

"Yes."

"Can't you tell——?"

"I'll meet you at the station."

Through the carriage window the lights of villages moved past. As[3] my anger with Roy for leaving me uncertain became sharper, the lights became circled in mist and passed increasingly slow. We stopped at a station; the fog whirled under its lamps. At last the platform. The red-brick walls shone in the translucency; as[4] I got out, the raw air caught at the throat.

Roy went quickly by, missing me in the crowd. I caught him by the arm. He turned and his face was serious and excited.

"Well?" I said.

"They're enquiring into some of George's and Jack's business. They questioned them this afternoon—and took away the accounts and books."

It sounded inevitable as I heard it. It sounded unlike news, it seemed something I had known for a long time.

"I couldn't say it on the telephone," Roy was talking fast, "my parents were too near."

C. P. Snow:

Strangers and Brothers (Faber and Faber, 1948)

[1] § **241.** 2.

[2] "down": can be omitted in the translation.

[3] *Comme? A mesure que?*

[4] "as." A gerund clause might be used; but see § **410.**, § **411.**

96

*QUESTIONED BY THE POLICE***

"Good evening," he said. "What can I do for you?"

The man in plain clothes took the initiative.

"Did you happen to walk through Chelsea Hospital gardens late this afternoon, sir?" he enquired. Both men were watching Fenton intently, and he realised that denial would be useless.

"Yes," he said, "yes, I did."

"You were carrying a parcel?"

"I believe I was."

"Did you put the parcel in a litter basket by the Embankment entrance, sir?"

"I did."

"Would you object to telling us what was in the parcel?"

"I have no idea."

"I can put the question another way, sir. Could you tell us where you obtained the parcel?"

Fenton hesitated. What were they driving at? He did not care for their method of interrogation.

"I don't see what it has to do with you," he said. "It's not an offence to put rubbish in a litter basket, is it?"

"Not ordinary rubbish," said the man in plain clothes.

Fenton looked from one to the other. Their faces were serious.

"Do you mind if I ask you a question?" he said.

"No, sir."

"Do you know what was in the parcel?"

"Yes."

"You mean the policeman here—I remember passing him on[1] the beat—actually followed me, and took the parcel after I had dropped[2] it in the bin?"

"That is correct."

"What an extraordinary thing to do. I should have thought he would have been better employed doing his regular job."

"It happens to be his regular job to keep an eye on people who behave in a suspicious manner."

Fenton began to get annoyed. "There was nothing suspicious in my behaviour whatsoever," he declared. "It so happens that I had been clearing up odds and ends in my office this afternoon, and it's rather a fad of mine to throw rubbish in the river on my way home. Very often I feed the gulls too. To-day I was about to throw in my usual packet when I noticed the officer here glance in my direction. It occurred to me that perhaps it's illegal to throw rubbish in the river, so I decided to put it in the litter basket instead."

The two men continued to stare at him.

"You've just stated," said the man in plain clothes, "that you didn't know what was in the parcel, and now you state that it was odds and ends from the office. Which statement is true?"

Fenton began to feel hunted.

DAPHNE DU MAURIER:
"The Alibi" from *The Breaking Point* (Gollancz, 1959)

[1] "on": "while he was on," etc. [2] § **82**.

97

*A STREET INCIDENT***

"Madam," I called out, "your hat is on fire."

She swung round and faced me with what Cockneys call a perishing look.

"Do you want me to give you in charge?" she asked sternly.

"If you take off your hat you'll see that it's on fire," I urged.

In those days a woman could not snatch her hat off her head. She had to pull out at least a couple of hat-pins first.

"You may think it very funny to try and make an April fool of a lady, but if you molest me any more I'll call a policeman to you."

It seemed to me that the wisp was perceptibly thicker, and I became so anxious that I hurried across[1] to a policeman on the other side of the road and told him I thought the woman's hat was on fire. She had continued on her way by this time, but from where we stood the smoke was clearly visible.

In those days, before the policemen of London all looked like Boy Scouts, a London bobby ran with considerable difficulty.

"You'd better run after her and tell[2] her again," he advised. "And I'll follow you."

I hurried off after the lady and assured her that her hat really was on fire. She swung round again, prepared to complain to the police of my behaviour when she saw the bobby advancing.

"Take off your hat, Mum. It's alight," he told her.

"How can my hat be alight?" she asked indignantly.

"Take it off, Mum, and you'll find out."

When she did, several of the flowers were smouldering, but the fag end of the cigarette had burnt itself out.

"This is a perfect mystery," she declared. I did not feel that the laws of chivalry demanded I should solve the mystery; instead I proffered my help to extinguish the glowing petals.

"I'm sorry I spoke so sharp to you, young man," she said. "But being April Fools' Day, I thought you was having a game with me."

We parted with mutual cordiality.

Sir Compton Mackenzie:

Sublime Tobacco (Chatto and Windus, 1957)

[1] "across." The sense of this word is carried by "on the other side of the road." Translate: "I hurried towards." [2] § **223**.

98

*THE NEW TEACHER—I**

I put on my coat and we went across to[1] the dark school.

"I wish you could[2] have seen it in sunshine," I said, "it looks much better."

"But I have,[3]" she said, to my surprise. "When I thought of applying I came over from Caxley and looked at the school and the village. I liked it all so much that that made up my mind for me. I know the neighbourhood fairly well through staying with friends. They have a good deal to do with the orchestra in Caxley."

"Do you play at all?"

"Yes, the violin and the piano. I should like to join the orchestra if it is easy to get in and out of Caxley."

The school was very still and unreal. The tidy rows of desks, the children's drawings, the pot of Roman hyacinths in flower on my desk all looked like stage properties awaiting the actors' presence to lend them validity. The artificial light heightened this effect.

'Miss Read':
Village School (Michael Joseph, 1955)

[1] Use two verbs to bring out the sense of "across" and "to."

[2] § **395**. 5.

[3] The ellipsis of the English cannot be repeated in the French. Clarify by completing the verb.

99

*THE NEW TEACHER—II**

Our shoes echoed noisily on the boards as we went through to the infants' room that would[1] be Miss Gray's own.

"I wonder *why*[2] they built the windows so horribly high!" exclaimed Miss Gray, looking at the narrow arches set up[3] in the wall. "Well, I know they didn't want the children to[4] look out, but really—such a peculiar mentality!"

She walked round her new domain, examining pictures and looking at books in the cupboards. Her pale face had grown quite pink with excitement and she looked almost pretty. It seemed a pity to take her away from it all, but if she had to catch the Caxley bus and we had to[5] face Mrs Pratt first, there was no time to spare.

"You are coming to us on the first of February, I believe?" I asked.

"Yes, it seems best. I've no notice to give in, but it means that I shall have just over a week to settle in the village, and it gives your supply teacher a little notice."

So we arranged that she would come over one day before the beginning of February to see about syllabuses, schemes of work, children's records, reading methods and all the other interesting school matters, but that now, with time pressing, we must hurry down the road to Mrs Pratt's house, before that lady began putting her two little children to bed.

'Miss Read':

Village School (Michael Joseph, 1955)

[1] *Serait* or *devait être*?
[2] Stress by an additional element in the French, not by italics.
[3] "high." [4] § **373**. [5] § **388**., § **399**.

100

*A GIRL DESCRIBES HER SCHOOLDAYS**

She told him her school was on the downs just behind Seaport: they had a French mistress called Mlle Dupont who had a vile temper. The headmistress could read Greek just like[1] English—Virgil. . . .

"I always thought Virgil was Latin."

"Oh yes. I meant Homer. I wasn't any good at Classics."

"Were you good at anything besides netball?"

"I think I was next best at maths, but I was never any good at trigonometry." In summer they went into Seaport and bathed, and every Saturday they had a picnic on the downs—sometimes a paper-chase on ponies, and once a disastrous affair on bicycles[2] which spread out over the whole county, and two girls didn't return till one in the morning. He listened fascinated, revolving the heavy gin in his glass without drinking.[3] The sirens squealed the All Clear through the rain, but neither of them paid[4] any attention. He said, "And then in the holidays you went back to Bury?"

Apparently her mother had died ten years ago, and her father was a clergyman attached in some way to the Cathedral. They had a very small house on Angel Hill.

Graham Greene:

The Heart of the Matter (Heinemann, 1948)

[1] Is the elliptic use of *comme* suitable here? See § **394**. 2.
[2] Show that it was the pupils who were on bicycles.
[3] Add "from it." [4] § **436**.

101

*TELEPHONE CONVERSATION**

"I know Viola," she said. "She's got a flat in Earl's Court Square. She's in the telephone book. If you like, I'll give her a ring tonight and tell her about you, and say you'll be calling her."

"I wish you would," I said. "It's the first time I've been[1] able to find anybody who might[2] know something about Janet Prentice."

"I'll do that," she said. "I'll tell her who you are."

"What would be a good time to ring her?" I enquired. "Does she work?"

"She works in a film studio," she said. "At Pinewood or some place like that. She does continuity, whatever that may mean. I should think you'd get her any evening at about seven o'clock—unless she's out, of course."

I thanked her, and at seven o'clock next morning I rang up Viola Dawson. "Miss Dawson," I said. "You won't know me—my name's Alan Duncan. I met a girl——"

"I know," she broke in. "Cynthia rang me. I've been expecting to hear from you, Mr Duncan."

"Good," I said. "What I really wanted to find out from you is if you know anything about Janet Prentice."

"I knew her quite well in the war," she said.

"You haven't seen her recently?"

"I haven't," she replied. "I'm not sure even where she's living now."

"I don't think she's[3] in England," I said. "I've been trying to find someone who could put me in touch with her." I paused, and then I said, "She was engaged to my brother, before he got killed."

"I know," she said. "I remember that happening."

"You do?"

"Oh yes. Janet and I were together at Beaulieu. We were great friends in those days, but I'm afraid I've lost touch with her now."

"Look, Miss Dawson," I said, "there's a lot I'd like to ask you about Janet. I never knew much about her, and I'm very anxious to get into touch with her if I can. Could we have a meal together, do you think?"

"I'd like to," she said.

"What about tonight? Have you eaten yet?"

She seemed to hesitate. "No—not yet. Yes, I could come tonight, a bit later on."

"Suppose[4] I call for you in about half an hour?"

NEVIL SHUTE:

Requiem for a Wren (Heinemann, 1955)

[1] § **382**. [2] § **384**. [3] § **374**. [4] *Si*.

102

*A BOARD MEETING****

From the position he had chosen right at the end of the Board table—the deliberately obscure class position of the obstreperous boy—Furness asked: "Does the item include the question of the General Manager's successor?"

"I think so, yes, certainly," said the Chairman, speaking as he always did at Board meetings, except about the most obvious matters, with his head turned only half to the front as though facing a biting wind, but in reality so that he could see any gesture of dissent or anger from the formidable figure of the Vice-Chairman at his side.

"Otherwise," said Furness ironically, "I see little point in the item. I suppose the General Manager *is* going to retire."

"Well, of course," said the Chairman, as though the question had raised a sudden doubt in his mind.

The Vice-Chairman said dryly: "I don't think Mr Furness is being entirely serious. He remembers, as we all do, the Board's decision two years ago to enforce retirement at sixty-five strictly in all cases—from General Manager down to office boy."

A fat, jolly director said: "How many office boys of sixty-five have we got?"

The Vice-Chairman did not deign to reply to this.

"The point about the item is," said Dillon irascibly, "as we all know in spite of these facetious remarks, that some of us would like to see Mr Matheson on the Board."

"Mr Chairman," called out Furness from a lolling position, "my question was not facetious."

"Of course not, Mr Furness," said the Chairman placatingly.

Dillon said, still in a bad temper: "It doesn't need me to say that Mr Matheson is a man of very wide building society experience, young for his years, who would be an asset to any building society board in the country. It would be a crying shame if our society were to lose his services at his comparatively early age." He was conscious that he had put his case far too soon in the discussion for it to make its full effect, and his puce face moved round suspiciously trying to pin down the conspiracy that had prematurely led him on.

ROY FULLER:
Image of a Society (André Deutsch, 1956)

103

*A WELL-TRAINED HUSBAND**

George Thorpe had always gone out on Saturday afternoon. His wife and daughter Muriel expected him to go out—to go to his club, or play golf or watch cricket matches, or whatever it was he did. When he went, they didn't ask where he was going, and when he came back, they didn't ask where he had been. They were comfortably indifferent to what George did, so long as he got out of the way. They liked the afternoon to themselves on Saturday; they liked to settle down in the sitting-room or the garden, according to the weather, and[1] knit and read and eat chocolates in peace.

Lately, however, George had shown a disinclination to go out, and they'd had to get him off in spite of himself.

"You'd better put your coat on today, George," said Mrs Thorpe at lunch one chilly Saturday.

"I didn't think of going out," said George, looking at the grey sky.

But after lunch Muriel brought his coat. She and her mother helped him into it and gave him his hat and kissed him.

"Enjoy yourself," said Mrs Thorpe, as she always did,[2] and when he had gone, Muriel slewed the sofa round to the sitting-room fire for her mother and drew up an armchair for herself.

They looked at George going down the drive—a familiar figure, stooping against the east wind, the fingers of one long, thin hand spread over the crown of his hat to keep it on.

"I don't know what's happened to him," said Muriel. "He seems to want to stay at home now[3] on Saturday afternoons."

"Well, he's not going to," said Mrs Thorpe, putting her feet up on the sofa. "Men should go out on Saturday afternoons, after they've been in their offices all week. He'd do nothing but fidget if he stayed in. He must keep up his interests."

"Oh, I'm all for it," said Muriel, opening a box of chocolates, although the lunch they had just finished had been hearty. "Have one?"

"Thanks," said her mother.

DOROTHY WHIPPLE:

"Saturday Afternoon" from *Pick of Today's Short Stories, No. 6* (Putnam, 1955)

[1] *Pour.* [2] § **223**. [3] § **333**.

104

*RETURN OF THE SOLDIER, 1915**

Hetty came in with a tray, on which was a loaf of white bread, a knife with[1] wooden handle cut in the pattern of a wheat-sheaf, salt and pepper castors, and a plate with two slices of cold mutton lying in its centre. She put them down.

"Now dear, try and eat, a little food will do you good."

He took up the knife with the cracked and blackened handle, the fork with the prongs straightened by himself after he had bent them using them as a harpoon on a stick. He looked at the cold mutton. Conscious of the two faces regarding his every movement, he got up and without a word went out of the room, and up the stairs to his bedroom.

Hetty looked at her younger daughter. "I expect[2] everything seems a bit strange to him, dear. Did you say anything to[3] upset him, when I was out of the room?"

"No, Mum, of course not."

"I expect he'll be all right soon. Perhaps, after his illness, the sight of cold mutton has put him off. I'll boil him an egg—put one on the gas, will you, dear, and make some toast—what a pity, I'd prepared some plaice for him, I expected your father with Phillip, I don't know why, and imagined us all having dinner together, as Phillip likes it to be called. Anyway, you boil the egg, Doris, and make some toast."

HENRY WILLIAMSON:
A Fox under my Cloak (Macdonald, 1955)

[1] § **282**. 3. (*c*).

[2] Distinguish between the two uses of "expect" found in this extract.

[3] "to": a relative clause will best translate the sense. See also § **381**., § **382**.

105

*MEETING IN PARIS**

She listened while he talked of his work and the Café Rieu, and, because he knew that none[1] of this was very interesting, he became irritated again.

"How can all this possibly interest you?" he asked.

"But of course it interests me," she said quietly, like a mother soothing a fractious child. "But I must be on my way back to my cousins. I am sorry, André, if I've wasted your time, but I just wanted to see you again. I can tell them all at home that you are happy and busy. They will like to know that. They haven't forgotten you, you know."

"I'm glad[2] you found me, Justine," he said, "and I hope[3] you'll enjoy your week in Paris."

As[4] they came out on to the pavement, he said:

"I'll walk with you to your bus."

"Oh, no," she said. "Back to your work. I've taken up too much of your time already.[5] Goodbye."

They shook hands. As she turned to walk away, he seemed to be about to say something, but did not do so. He watched her walk away. When she had gone some dozen paces he cried:

"Justine."

She turned again, so quickly that one might have thought she had been listening for[6] his voice. She came back towards him, and he went to meet her.

"You will be here for a week," he said. "We could meet again, if you would like that."

"I would like that, André," she said.

"Tell me the telephone number of your cousins—or their address."

She gave him the telephone number, and he scribbled it on an envelope.

J. B. Morton:
Springtime (Constable, 1956)

[1] Use *tout cela* with a negative construction. [2] § **379**.
[3] § **373**. [4] = "Just as." [5] Position in the French sentence?
[6] "for": use an infinitive construction.

106

*DISILLUSIONED MATURITY*****

She lifted her face and spoke gravely. "You are my friend," she said, "of course I care whether you are with me or not." He scrutinised her through half-closed lids. His face was haggard, gloomy with *ennui*. "How you harp on the word, you punctilious Jane. Do you suppose I am still in my teens? Twenty years ago, now—— It amuses me to hear you women talk. It's little you ever really feel."

"I don't think I am quite without feeling," she replied, "you are a little difficult, you know."

"Difficult," he echoed in derision. He checked himself and shrugged his shoulders. "You see, Jane, it's all on the surface; I boast of my indifference. It's the one rag of philosophy age denies no one. It is so easy to be mock-heroic—debonair, iron-grey, rhetorical, dramatic—you know it only too well, perhaps? But after all, life's comedy, when one stops smiling, is only the tepidest farce. Or the gilt wears off and the pinchbeck tragedy shows through. And so, as I say, we talk on, being past feeling. One by one our hopes come home to roost, our delusions find themselves out, and the mystery proves to be nothing but sleight-of-hand. It's age, my dear Jane—age; it turns one to stone. With you young people life's a dream; ask Nicholas here!" He shrugged his shoulders, adding under his breath, "But one wakes on a devilish hard pallet."

"Of course," said Jane slowly, "you are only talking cleverly, and then it does not matter whether it's true or not, I suppose. I can't say. I don't think you mean it, and so it comes to nothing. I can't and won't believe you feel so little—I can't." She continued to smile, yet, I fancied, with the brightness of tears in her eyes. "It's all mockery and make-believe; we are not the miserable slaves of time you try to fancy. There must be some way to win through." She turned away, then added slowly, "You ask me to be fearless, sincere, to speak my heart; I wonder, do you?"

My father did not look at her, appeared not to have seen the hand she had half held out to him, and as swiftly withdrawn.

WALTER DE LA MARE:

"The Almond Tree" from *Best Short Stories of Walter de la Mare* (Faber and Faber, 1945)

HISTORICAL AND POLITICAL

107

*LOCAL GOVERNMENT IN FRANCE***

To the British citizen, used to busy Borough and County Councils, meeting all the year round and, in the larger urban agglomerations, holding frequent committee meetings as well, it is evident that French local authorities, meeting as they do[1] for only a few weeks in the year, cannot have a similar range of activities. In fact, not only do French local Councils deal with fewer matters than are dealt with by British local authorities, but they also play a far less direct and responsible role in the running of local affairs.

To begin with, a number of functions which, in Britain, are the concern of local authorities are, in France, the direct responsibility of the state, although councillors sometimes serve on the state organs in the *département*. Education, for example, is a state service, controlled by officials of the ministry. Teachers are not local government employees, but civil servants. In towns with over 10,000 inhabitants, the police force is controlled (and largely paid for) by the state. In the rural areas, police duties are carried out by the gendarmerie, a military organisation directly responsible to the Ministry of War. The British citizen pays his rates to the Finance Department at the Town or County Hall. The Frenchman pays his local taxes to a tax-collector who is an official of the Ministry of Finance. A number of services are thus not 'local' at all in the British sense, but more nearly akin to local branches of the Ministry of National Insurance or the Post Office, the officials at the head of the local organisation being civil servants directly appointed by the minister and responsible to him. The Departmental Council has no responsibility in the matter (except to provide the money for the upkeep of buildings).

DOROTHY PICKLES:

France: the Fourth Republic (Methuen, 1955)

[1] Use a construction of the type referred to in § **222**. 1. or § **224**. (*c*); or say: "accustomed as they are to meeting" etc.

108

*THE BATTLE OF HASTINGS****

The king, therefore, drew up his force with the house-carls in front, forming the traditional shield-wall of the North—a thin line of armour, spears and axes, extending for about half a mile along the low, scrubby ridge. Behind them congregated the densely packed shire-levies, ready to assail the Normans when the house-carls had broken the first force of the attack. Harold himself, with the great flapping royal banner of Wessex, took his stand in the centre beside the hoar apple tree, just on the site of the abbey which William afterwards built to commemorate the battle.

The fight began at about nine o'clock. "The terrible sound of trumpets on both sides," wrote the Duke's chaplain, "signalled the start of battle." As soon as the Normans had deployed, their bowmen moved forward and, halting about a hundred yards from the English line, opened fire. Their technique, derived from the Vikings or possibly learnt from the Hungarian invasions of a century before, was not very advanced, their bows short, and their arrows flimsy. But the English, having scarcely any archers, could not reply and had to endure the flickering hail in patience. It did not, however, last long, for their assailants' ammunition was limited to what each man carried.

When, therefore, William's infantry moved forward to the attack, the shield-wall was still unbroken. "The English," we are told, "resisted valiantly, each man according to his strength, hurling back spears and javelins and weapons of all sorts, together with axes and stones fastened to pieces of wood." It was how they had always fought. The house-carls waited on the summit with their battle-axes poised over their heads and cracked open the skulls of every Norman who reached them. The Breton auxiliaries on the attackers' left—kinsmen of the Britons whom the English had defeated so often in the past—liked their reception so little that they fled down the hill. Many of the defenders, forgetting their king's orders, followed after them shouting in triumph.

At that moment there was nearly a panic in the Norman ranks. The rumour went round that the Duke had fallen, and there was a movement towards the rear. Then William, removing his helmet to show himself, galloped among the knights and rallied them. "He dominated the battle," wrote his chaplain, "bidding his men come with him more often than he ordered them to go in front of him." Wheeling his shaken squadrons, he launched a counter-attack against the pursuing and now breathless English. It was completely successful. In a static fight the Anglo-Saxons were still a match for anyone, but in mobility the trained Norman horsemen were far their superiors. The fyrdmen were cut down in hundreds, and few who had left the summit regained it.

ARTHUR BRYANT:
"Makers of the Realm" (*The Story of England*, Vol. 1)
(Collins, 1953)

109

*COAL IN BRITISH ECONOMY****

The importance of the coal industry in the nineteenth and twentieth centuries is universally recognised. Its prominence in earlier ages has been obscured by focussing attention upon the use of coal for smelting iron ore and neglecting its relation to other fields of economic activities. In mercantilist England coal had grown into general usage as the indispensable fuel of the householder, and it was extensively consumed in a great variety of industries. Confined in medieval times mainly to workers in metal (smiths) and lime-burners, it was subsequently adopted by others—bakers, brewers, brick-makers, calico-printers, casters of brass and copper, coopers, distillers, dyers, founders, glass-makers, pottery manufacturers, salt-makers, soap-boilers and sugar-refiners. It was employed in making iron wares though it was not suitable, on account of the sulphur in it, for smelting iron ore. A French traveller in 1738 termed coal "one of the greatest sources of English wealth and plenty" and "the soul of English manufactures"; and he expressly mentioned that lime which was burned with coal was widely applied as a fertiliser of the soil, and not merely for mortar in building, thus making coal an accessory of agriculture. In this way coal-mining was closely linked with the progress of numerous industries and with improved methods in farming. Its historical significance is reflected further in the contribution which it made to the evolution of a capitalist society, and in the influence exerted on public policy (especially as regards price regulation) in the interests of the consumer. In addition the transport of coal along the coast or to the Continent was an immense stimulus to shipping, since it accounted for a large proportion of the mercantile marine and nourished a 'nursery for seamen'; its conveyance from the pits to the river-side led to the invention of 'railways' in the sixteenth century; and the drainage of the mines gave birth to the steam engine in the seventeenth century.

E. LIPSON:

A Planned Economy or Free Enterprise (A. and C. Black, 1944)

110

*MODERN BUREAUCRACY***

When Conservatives cry "Away with control," they are often accused of a desire to relapse into chaos. What they mean is: "Do not imagine that you will create abundance by merely saying: 'Don't!'"

Moreover, they imply that the incredible tangle of modern administration is reaching the point, even without the addition of wartime controls, where production is inhibited.

How much national energy which might be usefully employed in and about[1] production is lavished upon the evasion of taxation—illegal or legitimate? Armies of accountants, representing some of our most intelligent brainpower, oceans of ink, whole forests of paper, platoons of barristers and solicitors, and a legion of fiscal G-men on the other side, inspectors, officials, and mathematicians engage constantly in the totally unproductive warfare of what[2] has become the great national industry of tax-dodging—or rather not an industry but an unseen brake, exhausting the efforts and wasting the time of the highest executives of all our real productive industries.

What is the more absurd is that the mass of tax payments are in reality largely a huge and unnecessary duplicating of contra-entries.

One set of men devise, print and publish a system of cards and insurance stamps representing in effect charges deducted as expenses from the taxable income of those who buy them. Countless women queue up at Post Offices to receive family allowances and other weekly payments, part of which are immediately repaid to the Treasury in income tax by their husbands, and officials both make, and receive, the payments in each case and carefully check, and audit, the accounts of both departments.

QUINTIN HOGG:

The Case for Conservatism (Penguin, 1947)

[1] Use a phrase to bring out the meaning of "about."

[2] Connect the elements of this mixed metaphor more naturally than is done in the English.

III

*EQUALITY AND LIBERTY EXAMINED*****

A static and immobile society of economic equality is not the environment in which the greatest number of persons can achieve the greatest possible development of the capacities of personality. Such achievement is a dynamic process which involves a dynamic society, with a rich variety of stations and functions and an easy movement of coming and going among those stations and functions. But to dismiss a general policy of economic equality is not for a moment to dismiss a policy of the progressive correction of economic inequality. On the contrary such a policy, as we have already seen, is a necessary corollary of legal equality, itself imperfect and unachieved as long as difference of economic means is such that it produces differences of civic standing and capacity. It is also a policy, as we have just seen, which is morally justified, and even morally demanded, in so far as the distribution of economic means is determined by factors and causes other than individual effort, and, more especially, by the factor of chance. The true policy of equality in the economic field is thus the correction of inequality, so far as such correction is demanded by the cause of legal equality, and so far as it is justified, and even demanded, by the action of factors other than effort in producing inequality in the distribution of means.

It remains to add that equality is not an isolated principle. It stands by the side of the principle of liberty and the principle of fraternity. It has to be reconciled with both, and, in particular, with the principle of liberty. Both liberty and equality matter; but there are reasons for thinking that liberty matters even more than equality. In its application and general extension it is, in our history, the older principle, asserted and vindicated in the course of struggles which now seem ancient history. But it is not by any means the stronger—on the contrary, it is rather the weaker—for being the older. It has not the vogue of fashion: it seems to be outmoded and outshone by the more recent star of equality. Yet the principle of liberty may still be argued to be the greater of the two. It is the greater because it is more closely connected with the supreme value of personality and the spontaneous development of its capacities.

SIR ERNEST BARKER:
Principles of Social and Political Theory (Oxford University Press, 1951)

112

*THE FIRST SESSION OF THE FIFTH REPUBLIC****

The three months parliamentary session, the first proper legislative sitting of Parliament under the Fifth Republic, ended this evening, when both chambers rose for the long summer recess.

The record of the session shows clearly enough that the desire of the Gaullist reformers to reduce and control the powers of Parliament—a desire which, as expressed in the constitution, received 80 per cent approval by the French electorate at the national referendum last year—has been realised most efficiently. Judging by the experience of the past three months, it is certainly not possible to go further than the opinion expressed recently by a political pamphleteer when he wrote that "the Fifth Republic is only faintly parliamentary, but it is so."

Part of the energies of both the National Assembly and the Senate has been spent in debating their own rules of procedure, and here the outcome has been that the severely limited powers of Parliament have been reduced still further. The irrevocable decision of the Constitutional Council—a sort of supreme court for settlement of constitutional disputes or points at issue—is such as to remove from the National Assembly any power, save the extreme one of a vote of censure, of harassing the Government.

The senate, the upper House, does not have even this power under the constitution, and partly because of this sense of impotence, the senators, who in their composition reflect much more the forces of the old Fourth Republic than the new political balance of the Fifth, have shown themselves a good deal more fractious and unready to accept the Government's views of the relationship between Executive and Legislature than has the National Assembly.

In the Assembly, the only issue which in the past three months has appeared to shake at least some of the deputies out of their lethargy has been that of the well worn question of State aid to church schools, which is apparently not as much of a dodo as some people think it ought to be. M. Debré's statement last Thursday, in which he promised to hasten the payment of existing credits for pupils at church schools, was a temporising and interim step which leaves the main issue unsettled.

"The French Assembly Reduced to a Debating Society"
from *The Times* of 28th July, 1959

113

*THE LOSING OF THE PEACE AFTER 1918**

Democracy failed to grasp—or in the persons of its statesmen even to apprehend—its historic opportunity in 1918–19. Though it is usually dangerous, on this occasion we may boldly speak of 'democracy' in general instead of particular democracies: because the war of 1914–18 was won by an alliance of the three great democracies of the world, Britain and the Dominions, France and America. Not one of these accepted responsibility for the creation of a new peaceful international society in Europe. First America, then Britain, retired into isolationism and moral superiority. America hid behind its ocean, Britain behind its Channel, in the shortsighted but unquestioned faith that their own democratic systems would endure in insulation from the political destiny of Europe. They accepted without criticism the political maxim of atomistic individualism, sometimes unfairly called liberalism, that the political institutions of a country were its own sole concern. It was understandable that the average American should have asked himself, even after being implicated in the greatest of European wars, what concern he had with Europe. It is much less intelligible that the average Briton should have adopted substantially the same attitude, of superiority and indifference.

Democracy in the post-war world[1] was the most substantial guarantee of peace: if only because the average man does not enjoy the prospect of war. One of the most constant of his incoherent and incompatible political desires[2] is the desire to avoid war. By far the best chance of maintaining the peace of Europe therefore lay in the establishment of democracy throughout Europe. By itself the establishment of democracy throughout Europe could not and would not have secured peace; because the basic contradiction between universal industrialisation and exclusive nationalism would still have remained. But the existence of democracy would have imposed a time-lag on recourse to the war-method: and that time-lag would have been infinitely precious, because it would have given a much greater opportunity to achieve the necessary changes of the *status quo* by consent.[3]

J. MIDDLETON MURRY:
Christocracy (Andrew Dakers, 1942)

[1] "in the post-war world": begin the sentence with this.

[2] "of his . . . desires": bring this phrase to the beginning of the sentence.

[3] "by consent": place immediately after the infinitive to which it refers.

114

*BRITISH FOREIGN POLICY BEFORE THE SECOND WORLD WAR****

It is not an exaggeration to say that it was not until Hitler seized power in Germany that the possible importance of Russia began to be weighed; and the contrast between the welcome given to Mussolini and the enthusiasm for his supposed achievements, and the obvious hope of Bolshevik failure at each stage of its development is, in retrospect, overwhelming. Even when it became obvious that the whole interest of Russia lay in peace, its government rarely received the consideration that was its due. After the outbreak of the Spanish Civil War, appeasement of Hitler was the main item on the programmes of most European powers. Not only did the British Government, for example, accept the destruction of Czechoslovakia as part of Hitler's price for peace; even after March 15, 1939, Mr Chamberlain, without consultation with Russia, took the risk of guaranteeing semi-fascist countries like Poland, Greece, and Rumania against aggression, while, at the same time, he made faint signs of a half-hearted desire to find terms upon which Russia would give aid in making possible the fulfilment of his guarantee. Yet it was common knowledge, at least from May, 1939, onwards, that while his second-class delegation to Moscow was leisurely negotiating there in an atmosphere made futile by Mr Chamberlain's acceptance of the Polish refusal to receive any aid from Russia which involved the presence of Russian troops upon its soil, he was also having conversations with German ministers which are largely unintelligible except as preparations for a still larger appeasement. Had he succeeded, Hitler would have been free to turn east and sweep through Poland into a full-scale attack upon Russia in the knowledge that he could count upon the neutrality of the Western powers and the probable aid of Japan. If the Russo-German Pact of August, 1939, was the necessary release of Hitler from the military danger of a war upon two fronts, it is vital to remember that Stalin merely achieved swiftly and successfully that relief from attack at the expense of the Western Powers which Mr Chamberlain was seeking slowly, and unsuccessfully, to achieve for the Western Powers at the expense of Soviet Russia.

HAROLD LASKI:

The Dilemma of our Times (Allen and Unwin, 1952)

115

*A DANGEROUS TREND IN DEMOCRACY*****

Human beings act in a great variety of irrational ways, but all of them seem to be capable, if given a fair chance, of making a reasonable choice in the light of available evidence. Democratic institutions can be made to work only if all concerned do their best to impart knowledge and to encourage rationality. But today, in the world's most powerful democracy, the politicians and their propagandists prefer to make nonsense of democratic procedures by appealing almost exclusively to the ignorance and irrationality of the electors. "Both parties," we were told in 1956 by the editor of a leading business journal, "will merchandise their candidates and issues by the same methods that business has developed to sell goods. These include scientific selection of appeals and planned repetition. . . . Radio spot announcements and ads will repeat phrases with a planned intensity. Bill-boards will push slogans of proven power. . . . Candidates need, in addition to rich voices and good diction, to be able to look 'sincerely' at the TV camera."

The political merchandisers appeal only to the weaknesses of voters, never to their potential strength. They make no attempt to educate the masses into becoming fit for self-government; they are content merely to manipulate and exploit them. For this purpose all the resources of psychology and the social sciences are mobilised and set to work. Carefully selected samples of the electorate are given 'interviews in depth.' These interviews in depth reveal the unconscious fears and wishes most prevalent in a given society at the time of an election. Phrases and images aimed at allaying or, if necessary, enhancing these fears, at satisfying these wishes, at least symbolically, are then chosen by the experts, tried out on readers and audiences, changed or improved in the light of the information thus obtained. After which the political campaign is ready for the mass communicators. All that is now needed is money and a candidate who can be coached to look 'sincere.' Under the new dispensation, political principles and plans for specific action have come to lose most of their importance. The personality of the candidate and the way he is projected by the advertising experts are the things that really matter.

ALDOUS HUXLEY:

Brave New World Revisited (Chatto and Windus, 1959)

116

*JUSTICE UNDER ELIZABETH I****

In the domain of treason, under Elizabeth, the reign of law was, in effect, superseded, and its place was taken by a reign of terror.

It was in the collection of evidence that the mingled atrocity and absurdity of the system became most obvious. Not only was the fabric of a case often built up on the allegations of the hired creatures of the Government, but the existence of the rack gave a preposterous twist to the words of every witness. Torture was constantly used; but whether, in any particular instance, it was used or not, the consequences were identical. The threat of it, the hint of it, the mere knowledge in the mind of a witness that it might at any moment be applied to him—

those were differences merely of degree; always, the fatal compulsion was there, inextricably confusing truth and falsehood. What shred of credibility could adhere to testimony obtained in such circumstances—from a man, in prison, alone, suddenly confronted by a group of hostile and skilful examiners, plied with leading questions, and terrified by the imminent possibility of extreme physical pain? Who could disentangle among his statements the parts of veracity and fear, the desire to placate his questioners, the instinct to incriminate others, the impulse to avoid, by some random affirmation, the dislocation of an arm or a leg? Only one thing was plain about such evidence: it would always be possible to give to it whatever interpretation the prosecutors might desire. The Government could prove anything. It could fasten guilt upon ten innocent men with the greatest facility. And it did so, since by no other means could it make certain that the one actual criminal—who might be among them—should not escape. Thus it was that Elizabeth lived her life out, unscathed; and thus it happened that the glories of her age could never have existed without the spies of Walsingham, the damp cells of the Tower, and the notes of answers, calmly written down by cunning questioners, between screams of agony.

LYTTON STRACHEY:
Elizabeth and Essex (Chatto and Windus, 1928)

117

*FAMOUS DEVALUATIONS*****

The silver coinage of which we recently took leave had long been a 'token' coinage, that is to say, its nominal value bore no relation to its intrinsic value as metal, and its composition might therefore be altered at will without any effect upon its face value or purchasing power. By contrast, in the sixteenth century the only sound currency was one in which the face value of the coins corresponded fairly closely to their intrinsic value, and for a government to interfere with the metallic content was thus to upset not only the currency but the values and prices expressed in it. This is not to say that such action was never justified. On the contrary, throughout the later Middle Ages the ever-widening disparity between the available stock of precious metal and the volume of business transactions which it was called upon to 'carry' made the periodic reminting of this metal into a greater sum of money, and a corresponding reduction in the metallic content of each coin, practically unavoidable. Edward IV's recoinage of 1461 had been the last of this series of enforced debasements. Wolsey, when he debased the coinage in 1526, could scarcely plead the same exigency; but even his alteration of the weight (although not of the fineness) of the silver coins can be looked upon as a defensive measure dictated by a war-time fall in the exchanges and the resulting drain of metal out of the country. Neither plea, nor indeed any other, can be put in with regard to the Great Debasement of the 'forties. The country was not short of silver; indeed, the amount in circulation had lately been augmented by a considerable quantity of monastic silver. Nor was the exchange-outlook unfavourable; the pound sterling had been steadily appreciating for a decade, and the tendency was for silver to flow into, not out of, the country. Henry VIII's bedevilment of the currency, which would itself reverse these favourable trends, answered to no national interest save that which attached to governmental solvency.

S. T. Bindoff:

"Tudor England" (*The Pelican History of England*, Vol. v) (Penguin, 1950)

118

*THE BRITISH VICTORY IN AFRICA**

Horrocks went over to the First Army and staged the corps attack on Tunis on the 6th May; it was made in great strength at the selected point and broke clean through the enemy defences to the west of Tunis. Bizerta and Tunis were captured on the 7th May and the enemy was then hemmed in to the Cap Bon peninsula.

The first troops to enter Tunis were those of our own 7th Armoured Division. They had earned this satisfaction. Organised enemy resistance ended on the 12th May, some 248,000 being taken prisoner.

And so the war in Africa came to a close. It ended in a major disaster for the Germans; all their troops, stores, dumps, heavy weapons, and equipment were captured. From a purely military point of view the holding out[1] in North Africa once the Mareth Line had been broken through, could never be justified. I suppose Hitler ordered it for political reasons. It is dangerous to undertake tasks which are militarily quite unsound, just for political reasons; it may sometimes be necessary, but they will generally end in disaster.

The contribution of the Eighth Army to the final victory in North Africa had been immense. It drove Rommel and his army out of Egypt, out of Cyrenaica, out of Tripolitania, and then helped the First Army to finish them off in Tunisia. Only first-class troops could have done it, and I realised what an honour and what an excitement it was to command such a magnificent army at the time of its greatest triumphs.

LORD MONTGOMERY:
Memoirs (Collins, 1958)

[1] Use an infinitive or a noun.

119

*A CRITICAL MOMENT IN WORLD AFFAIRS***

Late in the night of February 20 a telephone message reached me as I sat in my old room at Chartwell (as I often sit now) that[1] Eden had resigned. I must confess that my heart sank, and for a while the dark waters of despair overwhelmed me. In a long life I have had many ups and downs. During all the war soon to come and in its darkest times I never had any trouble in sleeping. In the crisis of 1940, when so much responsibility lay upon me, and also at many very anxious, awkward moments in the following five years, I could always flop into bed and go to sleep after the day's work was done—subject of course to any emergency call. I slept sound and awoke refreshed, and had no feelings except appetite to grapple with whatever the morning's boxes might bring. But now on this night of February 20, 1938, and on this occasion only, sleep deserted me. From midnight till dawn I lay in my bed consumed by emotions of sorrow and fear. There seemed one strong young figure standing up against long, dismal, drawling tides of drift and surrender, of wrong measurements and feeble impulses. My conduct of affairs would have been different from his in various ways; but he seemed to me at this moment to embody the life-hope of the British nation, the grand old British race that had done so much for men and had yet some more to give. Now he was gone. I watched the daylight slowly creep in through the windows, and saw before me in mental gaze the vision of Death.

Sir Winston S. Churchill:
"The Gathering Storm" (*The Second World War*, Vol. 1) (Cassell, 1948)

[1] Use a phrase linking the conjunction to the main verb.

120

*THE DESTRUCTION OF THE STALIN MYTH****

The last anniversary of Stalin's death passed completely unnoticed in the Soviet press. But there still are countless pictures of him in hotels and even in governmental offices, some of them showing with revolting hypocrisy the elder Lenin handing over to him the baton of power, and countless silver-painted statues of him in the bleak, threadbare little parks and gardens all over the Soviet Union. The names of cities like Stalingrad, Stalinabad, and Stalinsk have not been changed. The smart, shiny locomotives on the big express trains still carry resplendent plaques showing Lenin and Stalin, in a halo of stars. Khrushchev made it quite clear in his speech that the transformation of names, emblems, and the like would have to go slowly, and that most old names would not be affected, which was reasonable enough. To take Stalin out of everything would be an

Augean job. To mention just one item—if his name were to be absolutely obliterated, millions upon millions of books would have to be scrapped, including children's books, poems, and songs.

But a good deal has been done, if not actually to erase all evidence of him, to play down his role. Surviving members of his family are seldom seen, and in fact are ostracised. For years a group of galleries in the Pushkin Museum was stuffed with gifts he had received, particularly those which arrived from all over the world on his seventieth birthday; these have been relegated inconspicuously to back rooms in the Museum of the Revolution. He has been cut from the name of the Marx-Engels-Lenin-Stalin Institute (also for some reason Engels has been dropped) and, even if actual cities have not been renamed, many lesser entities like factories and institutes are now known by some other name. In at least one airport, where enormous frescoes of Lenin and Stalin stood on opposite walls of the reception hall, that of Stalin has been ripped out; nothing replaces him, and the whole wall is an angry scar. Perhaps most interesting of all, the Stalin Peace Awards have been renamed the International Lenin Prizes for Strengthening Peace among Peoples. It was also announced in September, 1956, that the Lenin Prizes for achievement in science, literature, art, and, so on, would be 'revived.'

JOHN GUNTHER:
Inside Russia Today (Hamish Hamilton, 1958)

121

*THE REASONS FOR THE GENERAL ELECTION, 1951****

We had carried on now for eighteen months with an exiguous majority. The strain on our Members, some of whom were in indifferent health, was very great. It was not pleasant to have Members coming from hospital at the risk of their lives to prevent a defeat in the House. The Opposition tactics were designed to wear out our Members by keeping them late every night. This was done particularly by putting down 'Prayers' against Orders. These come on after the ordinary business of the day. Many of our Members lived in the outer suburbs. It was easy, therefore, for Conservatives who resided in central London to keep things going until last buses and trains had gone. It only needed a breakdown in health of half a dozen of our Members to put us in a minority.

I had therefore to consider when it would be necessary to appeal to the country. At the moment we had a favourable balance of payments, but I was well aware how precarious was the situation. There was the impact of the heavy rearmament programme which would inevitably mean some halt in our progress toward a better standard of life. We required more adequate support in the House if we were to face successfully these difficulties. There was a further reason. The late King and his Queen were to visit Australia and New Zealand in the spring of 1952. It would, I knew, be a constant anxiety to the King if there were a possibility of a fall of the Government or a General Election during his absence from the country. Clearly therefore there were cogent reasons for having an Election in the autumn and I made up my mind before the House rose for the Autumn Recess. It will be seen that there is no foundation for the silly suggestions of some Tory Members that we had an Election in order to get out of our responsibilities.

C. R. ATTLEE:
As It Happened (Heinemann, 1954)

122

*DEMOCRATIC VALUES IN FRANCE***

The values and outlook of the liberal democratic tradition are firmly rooted in France. The instinctive suspicion of men in power, despite its dangers, is a safeguard of the liberty of the subject, and a far healthier attitude than that of automatic obedience. The French voter belies his superficial contempt for politics by the extent to which he uses his civic rights—the proportion[1] going to the polls is almost as high as in Britain, and far higher than in the United States. Magistrates remain honest and independent of the executive—on a far lower salary scale than their British *confrères*. Racial tolerance is in many respects more general and more widespread than it is[2] across the Atlantic, or even across the Channel.

French democracy faces much more immediate external and internal dangers than[3] either Britain or the United States. The barrier of the sea may have lost its military value to-day; it has not lost its psychological importance. The strength of the French Communist party presents a challenge which confronts none of the other traditional democracies. Yet the French have preserved their sense of proportion. The democratic decencies survive: freedom of speech, of assembly, and of organisation; impartial judicial treatment even for those whom most Frenchmen regard as public enemies; fair elections. In spite of the difficulties arising from the heritage of the past, the ordinary Frenchman clings with remarkable determination and fidelity to the democratic ideal.

PHILIP WILLIAMS:

Politics in Post-War France (Longmans, Green, 1954)

[1] Add "of the electors." [2] § **277**. 6. [3] § **154**.

123

*THE FALL OF JAPAN***

There were some in America who believed that Japan's downfall could have been achieved more economically by a greater use of air-power[1] from bases in China, and possibly Siberia. They maintained that her sea communications could have been severed and her power of resistance in the homeland destroyed just as effectively by air action alone, without a long and costly approach[2] by sea as a prelude to invasion. The more advanced exponents of air-power maintained that political objectives elsewhere, in Burma, Malaya, and the East Indies, might have been[3] renounced for the time being and could have been attained without fighting once the air battle had been won.[4] The American Chiefs of Staff had rejected these ideas.

It would be a mistake to suppose[5] that the fate of Japan was settled by the atomic bomb. Her defeat was certain before the first bomb fell, and was brought about by overwhelming maritime power. This alone[6] had made it possible to seize ocean bases from which to launch the final attack and force her metropolitan Army to capitulate without striking a blow. Her shipping had been destroyed. She had entered the war with over five and a half million tons, later much augmented by captures and new construction, but her convoy system and escorts were inadequate and ill-organised. Over eight and a half million tons of Japanese shipping were sunk, of which five million fell to submarines. We, an island Power, equally dependent on the sea, can read the lesson and understand[7] our own fate had we failed to master the U-boats.

SIR WINSTON S. CHURCHILL:
"Triumph and Tragedy" (*The Second World War*, Vol. VI) (Cassell, 1954)

[1] *armements aériens.*

[2] "long and costly approach." The phrase needs adjusting. Use an infinitive construction. Bring out the exact meaning of "costly."

[3] Use the active voice in the French.

[4] "once the air battle," etc. Put this clause before the main verb "could have been attained." See also § **409**.

[5] § **377**.

[6] "This alone." Say: "This power alone."

[7] Add: "what would have been."

124

*SCEPTICISM IN THE EIGHTEENTH CENTURY***

It is true that, in the early years of George III's reign, there were Britons of the intellectual calibre of Hume and Gibbon who were avowed sceptics. Yet even Gibbon thought well to veil his real thought in the decent obscurity of the ironical. And as every reader of Boswell's *Johnson* is aware, these great sceptics and their lesser followers were[1] ill spoken of in society, while the batteries opened upon them by orthodox writers were overwhelming in quantity, though no longer[2] in quality. In 1776, a date usually regarded in retrospect as belonging to the period most marked by infidelity and laxity of doctrine, Hume wrote to Gibbon about the reception of the first part of his Roman history, "the prevalence of superstitition in England prognosticates the fall of philosophy and the decay of taste." Hume was too pessimistic, but he was speaking from real experience.

In any case the scholarly[3] scepticism of the English Eighteenth Century was addressed only to a highly educated audience. Its optimistic philosophy was the outcome of upper-class conditions of life. When, in the period of the French Revolution, Tom Paine appealed to the multitude on behalf of Deism as the proper creed of democracy, a new age had arrived. In the lifetime of the fastidious and conservative Gibbon, it has been said that infidelity, like hair-powder, could only be worn by the aristocracy. The mass of the nation was either actively or passively Christian, accepting the religion that it was taught. The lowest strata of society had indeed been taught nothing at all, but these also the Charity Schools and the Wesleyan mission were striving to raise out of ignorance to[4] the mental level of understanding Christians.

G. M. TREVELYAN:

English Social History (Longmans, Green, 1944)

[1] Use a construction with the active voice.
[2] "though no longer": expand and clarify.
[3] ="of scholars."
[4] "to": translate by a verb.

125

*THE WESTERN ACHIEVEMENT*****

On this view then—a humble view and yet a proud view too—the main strand of our modern Western history is not the parish-pump politics of our Western society as inscribed on triumphal arches in a half-dozen parochial capitals or recorded in the national and municipal archives of ephemeral 'Great Powers.' The main strand is not even the expansion of the West over the world—so long as we persist in thinking of that expansion as a private enterprise of the Western society's own. The main strand is the progressive erection, by Western hands, of a scaffolding within which all the once separate societies have built themselves into one. From the beginning, mankind has been partitioned; in our day we have at last become united. The Western handiwork that has made this union possible has not been carried out with open eyes, like David's unselfish labours for the benefit of Solomon; it has been performed in heedless ignorance of its purpose, like the labours of the animalcula that build a coral reef up from the bottom of the sea till at length an atoll rises above the waves. But our Western-built scaffolding is made of less durable materials than that. The most obvious ingredient in it is technology, and man cannot live by technology alone. In the fullness of time, when the oecumenical house of many mansions stands firmly on its own foundations and the temporary Western technological scaffolding falls away—as I have no doubt that it will—I believe it will become manifest that the foundations are firm at last because they have been carried down to the bedrock of religion.

We have reached the Pillars of Hercules and it is time to draw in sail, for we cannot see clearly very much farther ahead. In the chapter of history on which we are now entering, the seat of material power is moving at this moment still farther away from its pre-da Gaman locus. From the small island of Britain, lying a stone's throw from the Atlantic coast of the continent of Asia, it is moving to the larger island of North America, a bow-shot farther distant. But this transfer of Poseidon's trident from London to New York may prove to have marked the culmination of the dislocating effects of our current Oceanic age of intercommunication; for we are now passing into a new age in which the material medium of human intercourse is going to be neither the Steppe nor the Ocean, but the Air, and in an air age mankind may succeed in shaking its wings free from their fledgeling bondage to the freakish configuration of the surface—solid or liquid—of the globe.

ARNOLD TOYNBEE:

Civilisation on Trial (Oxford University Press, 1948)

CHARACTERS AND PORTRAITS

126

*PORTRAIT OF CLEMENT ATTLEE****

First, regard the man. In appearance he is undistinguished. He would go unremarked among the hosts of professional men journeying to the City any morning. A solicitor or chartered accountant might be the verdict. His modesty is no pose. Sir Winston Churchill is reputed to have said in a roguish moment that he has a lot to be modest about, and Mr Attlee behaves exactly as if the jest were true. Modesty could hardly go farther. It is almost staggering in a politician. His voice is thin and unmusical. For speech-making as an art he cares not a fig. He is without what the French call the long breath. He usually says what he wants to say in half an hour. He is direct, positive, unemotional. The hatred of social injustice which has influenced all his public action is seated in the reason, not the heart as with so many Labour men. No soul-animating eloquence has escaped from him on the themes of poverty or unemployment. He is as incapable of demagogy as a poker. He is not an intellectual. On the contrary, he reserves a smile for the Labour intelligentsia, some of whom, he says in his autobiography, "can be trusted to take a wrong view of any subject."

Altogether you would have said he was endowed with every natural disqualification for the leadership of a party, especially the Labour Party, and to the natural handicaps must be added the social one of birth. He is sprung from the well-to-do middle class, was inclined to Toryism as a young man, but suffered a slow conversion in his twenties to an empirical socialism. And yet here he is, having led the Labour Party for twenty years short of a few months, and for six of them he has been Labour Prime Minister! The granting of independence to India would alone have lent historical significance to his Premiership. The completing of the edifice of the Welfare State and the creation of the National Health Service guarantee its historical pre-eminence in the social field. The nationalisation of the railways, mines, electricity, and gas was the first large instalment the country has had of the practical socialism which is his gospel. Proof of a larger statesmanship is furnished by his acceptance of conscription and a large rearmament programme as the inescapable obligation of a British Government confronted by the Russian menace. To have brought his party to accept this against all instincts and in opposition to its whole philosophy could never have been done by the tame mouse of a man of some people's imaginings. Sir Winston Churchill has never ceased to applaud the courage and wisdom of it.

HARRY BOARDMAN:
"Mr Attlee" from *The Manchester Guardian* (1953)

127

*THE COMPLEXITIES OF MODERN INVENTIONS***

It was the world that was absent-minded and it was Pnin whose business it was to set it straight. His life was a constant war with insensate objects that fell apart, or attacked him, or refused to function, or viciously got themselves lost as soon as they entered the sphere of his existence. He was inept with his hands to a rare degree;[1] but because he could manufacture in a twinkle a one-note mouth organ out of a pea pod, make a flat pebble skip ten times on the surface of a pond, shadowgraph with his knuckles a rabbit (complete with blinking eye), and perform a number of other tame tricks that Russians have up their sleeves, he believed himself endowed with considerable manual and mechanical skill.[2] On gadgets he doted with a kind of dazed, superstitious delight. Electric devices enchanted him. Plastics swept him off his feet. He had a deep admiration for the zipper. But the devoutly plugged-in clock would make nonsense of his mornings after a storm in the middle of the night had paralysed the local power station. The frame of his spectacles would snap in mid-bridge, leaving him with two identical pieces, which he would vaguely attempt to unite, in the hope, perhaps, of some organic marvel of restoration coming to the rescue.

VLADIMIR NABOKOV:

Pnin (Heinemann, 1957)

[1] A phrase such as *on ne peut plus* could be used. Remember that adverbial phrases normally cling to the main verb in French.

[2] "manual skill" = *dextérité*.

128

*AN IRISH WASHERWOMAN**

I toyed with games, and enjoyed kicking a ball gently before me along the pavement, but when I discovered that any boy who joined me grew violent and started to push and kick, I took a dislike to games as well. I preferred little girls because they didn't fight so much, but otherwise I found them insipid and lacking in any solid basis of learning. The only[1] women I cared for were grown-ups, and my most intimate friend was an old washerwoman called Miss Cooney who had been in the lunatic asylum and was very religious. It was she who had made me feel sorry for dogs. She would run a mile after anyone she saw hurting an animal and even go to the police about them. The police never paid any attention to her because they knew she was mad. She was a sad-looking woman with grey hair, high cheek-bones and toothless gums. While she ironed, I would sit[2] for hours in the hot, damp kitchen, turning over the pages of her religious books. She was very fond of me, too, and told me she was sure I would be a priest when I grew up. I agreed that I might be a bishop but I wasn't sure. I told her there were so many other things that I couldn't tell what I'd be eventually, but I could see she didn't quite know what I meant. Miss Cooney thought there was only one thing a genius could be and that was[3] a priest.

FRANK O'CONNOR:

"The Genius" from *Winter's Tales I* (Macmillan, 1955)

[1] § **382**. [2] *Cf.* § **116**. 2. *Note* (*c*).

[3] "and that was": can be omitted in the translation.

129

*PORTRAIT OF A YOUNG MAN**

Robert has come back from his ten-year exile, both better and worse. His manners have improved. He is more polite. But I feel that he is, in reality, more pig-headed than ever. Almost as pig-headed as his mother, in her worst days. You can see it in his face, even when he smiles.

I was shocked when I first saw Robert, on his return. At twenty-eight, he looks like forty. His face is like a peasant's,[1] thin and hard, coloured like the inside of an old rein; and seamed as if by cuts.

But even when he does not smile, he has always a smiling air. He has the habitual expression that I saw once on the face of a successful young pugilist, at Paddington Station. He was going to some fight in the north, and he was surrounded by a group of admirers, who continually talked about his prowess, not to him, but across him, reminding each other[2] of his feats, and illustrating his blows; as, I am told, the courtiers of some barbarous chief flatter him, not directly, but to[3] each other, surrounding him with a glory which seems to him, since he contributes nothing to its production, like the natural and proper atmosphere of royalty.

Robert has the little smile of that scarred[4] young boxer; at once melancholy and knowing; as if he said "All the same, I do the fighting."

An obstinate smile, which alarms me. But I am resolved not to quarrel with Robert. And when now he remarked, in his usual way, that some of the trees in the drive were pretty rotten and ought to come down, I answered only, "They'll last my time at Tolbrook," and changed the subject.

JOYCE CARY:
To be a Pilgrim (Michael Joseph, 1942)

[1] § **193**. (*b*). [2] § **251**. 7.
[3] Use a gerundive construction.
[4] "scarred." Translate: "with the scarred face."

130

*EVOCATION OF A FEMALE CHARACTER*****

Half an hour ago the mistress of the house, Isabella Tyson, had gone down the grass path in her thin summer dress, carrying a basket, and had vanished, sliced off by the gilt rim of the looking-glass. She had gone presumably into the lower garden to pick flowers; or as it seemed more natural to suppose, to pick something light and fantastic and leafy and trailing, travellers' joy, or one of those elegant sprays of convolvulus that twine round ugly walls and burst here and there into white and violet blossoms. She suggested the fantastic and the tremulous convolvulus rather than the upright aster, the starched zinnia, or her own burning roses alight like lamps on the straight posts of their rose trees. The comparison showed how very little, after all these years, one knew about her; for it is impossible that any woman of flesh and blood of fifty-five or sixty should be really a wreath or a tendril. Such comparisons are worse than idle and superficial—they are cruel even, for they come like the convolvulus itself trembling between one's eyes and the truth. There must be truth; there must be a wall. Yet it was strange that after knowing her all these years one could not say what the truth about Isabella was; one still made up phrases like this about convolvulus and travellers' joy. As for facts, it was a fact that she was a spinster; that she was rich; that she had bought this house and collected with her own hands—often in the most obscure corners of the world and at great risk from poisonous stings and Oriental diseases—the rugs, the chairs, the cabinets which now lived their nocturnal life before one's eyes. Sometimes it seemed as if they knew more about her than we, who sat on them, wrote at them, and trod on them so carefully, were allowed to know. In each of these cabinets were many little drawers, and each almost certainly held letters, tied with bows of ribbon, sprinkled with sticks of lavender or rose leaves. For it was another fact—if facts were what one wanted—that Isabella had known many people, had had many friends; and thus if one had the audacity to open a drawer and read her letters, one would find the traces of many agitations, of appointments to meet, of upbraidings for not having met, long letters of intimacy and affection, violent letters of jealousy and reproach, terrible final words of parting—for all these interviews and assignations had led to nothing—that is, she had never married, and yet, judging from the mask-like indifference of her face, she had gone through twenty times more of passion and experience than those whose loves are trumpeted forth for all the world to hear.

VIRGINIA WOOLF:
A Haunted House (The Hogarth Press, 1944)

131

*A FILM IDOL***

It was the women who went for Barry. They adored the way he stood there on the stage, in his English clothes, with his hands clenched. It was strange it had meant so little to the women in England. . . .

In a matter of months his face was more familiar to women all over the world than that of their own husbands. And the husbands did not mind. In a sense, it was a sort of compliment if a girl married a chap at all. It must mean that the chap they married was a super-Barry. His hat—a trilby with a dent in it—his cigarette, never hanging[1] from his lips but always held between his fingers, the little scar on the side of the temple that suggested a brush with a rhino or a knife thrown in a Shanghai joint (in fact he had slipped on the breakwater at Herne Bay when he was not looking)—it all exercised a subtle and indefinable magic which left every other movie star standing at the post. But above all it was the mouth, firm and decisive above that square jaw with the cleft in the chin, which maddened millions. It never relaxed, it never smiled, it never, in fact, did anything. That was what got them. Women were weary of close-ups of their favourite stars lip-to-lip in a passionate embrace, and Barry did not give them that. Instead, he turned away. Or stared over the girl's shoulder. Or just murmured the word "You!" and nothing else. Then there would be a fade-out into the next scene, and the fans would be left writhing.

DAPHNE DU MAURIER:

The Breaking Point (Gollancz, 1959)

[1] See § **116**. 2. *Note* (*c*).

132

*AN ASPIRING CIVIL SERVANT*****

Balliol Gonville was a gangling etiolated fellow who looked misleadingly as if his formative years had been darkened by the shadow of too much improving literature. His university studies had in fact been interrupted for two terms after he had been caught one night climbing out of the wrong window, but despite this setback he not only found time to bat regularly for his college but also had edited one of those cloistered periodicals upon whose cuttlefish pages so many gestating Sunday critics have sharpened their embryonic beaks.

He had never set his boyhood sights on being an engine driver and after seriously considering with a degree of undergraduate socialism the high wages earned by unskilled but well organised labour, Gonville had decided in his second university year to enter the Civil Service. Like many other aspirants, he made the decision without fully understanding its nature. Although the vocation sounded an excitingly responsible one, his working knowledge of the functions of a public servant was limited to the hoary but ever popular collection of weak humour based on tea-cups, red tape and wordy equivocation.

His choice was sealed by the visit to his university of a Ministry of Labour official who was sadly sifting the students in search of likely candidates. Being of outstanding academic ability, Gonville was an obvious choice (in fact he was the only student so chosen) and he sat successfully for the Civil Service written examination. Then, displaying the degree of hopeful enterprise and painstaking research which boded well for his future as an administrator, he had turned up for the subsequent interview armed with prefabricated answers to most of the questions asked at such interviews over the previous five years.

MATTHEW FINCH:

Hang your Hat on a Pension (Dennis Dobson, 1958)

133

*PROFESSOR CAIRNS***

Professor Cairns was a great shaggy man, very careless of his dress and appearance, with a brooding powerful face. His children collected stories of his absence of mind and used to tease and amuse him by asking him to correct or verify them. If a ticket collector came to his compartment on the train he would as like as not grasp the hand held out for his ticket and shake it warmly and pass the time of day, and then carry on his talk with his travelling companions. A few years after the tragically early death of his wife he called at our manse with a message for my father. My mother asked him to stay for tea but he excused himself saying: "My wife will be expecting me at home." My mother was heart-struck, imagining the fresh pang of bereavement[1] when he stepped over his own threshold and remembered. Yet it may have been an even deeper forgetfulness in which the excuse from the past slipped back into the past as soon as he had made it.

When he did stay to tea his conversation was rich and original, full of varied knowledge, and so stimulating that my father himself glowed and talked as at no other time. In spite of these visits, and mine to play with his children, Alison and David, I never expected him to know me in the street. His deep eyes under their wild brows had the appearance of piercing through everything material to the truths and visions that absorb a prophet. But he always stopped. He would even cross the road if I walked on the other side. Then a little ritual was performed. He tapped my shoulder while I fidgeted a little and smiled self-consciously. His voice rumbled up from the deeps of his heavy ulster, his muffler, coat and waistcoat. "Be virtuous," he said, "and you will be happy." Then he hurried on with an enigmatic gleam in his eyes. He knew that I did not believe it; he may even have doubted it himself, but at least the converse was true.

LYN IRVINE:

So much Love, so little Money (Faber and Faber, 1957)

[1] Modify for translation purposes: e.g., "the fresh pang he would feel when . . . and remembered his bereavement."

134

*A SUCCESSFUL DOCTOR IN A WORKING-CLASS DISTRICT****

That same evening, at six, and thereafter on three nights of the week, I attended at the surgery in Trongate Cross. When I arrived the waiting-room was always packed to the door with patients—women in shawls, ragged children, workmen from the docks—and the hectic session which followed often ran on until eleven o'clock at night, after which there were usually one or two urgent calls which Thompson, the dispenser, gave me as he finally closed up. It was hard work. Dr Mathers had been guilty of no exaggeration when he spoke of his enormous practice. I soon found that he had an extraordinary reputation amongst the poor people who inhabited this slum district.

His fiery personality alone gave him great prestige, and his methods were abrupt, forceful, and dramatic. He had an instinct for diagnosis and did not hesitate to give his opinion, usually in the broad vernacular. He never spared himself, worked like a galley slave, and bullied his people a good deal. They liked him for it. His prescriptions were drastic. He used the maximum dose of every drug, and a patient who had been severely purged or violently sweated would remark with a knowing shake of his head: "Ay, there's something *in* the wee doctor's medicine."

Mathers was sensitive about his diminutive stature, yet he had all the vanity of the small man, and thoroughly enjoyed his success. He loved to feel that he could triumph where the neighbouring doctors failed, and would chuckle over a case where he had 'wiped the eye' of one of his colleagues. But most of all he delighted in the fact that from this drab little surgery, in a poor-class district, with no more than a Conjoint diploma, he was able to reside in style in a large villa in the suburbs, to run a Sunbeam car, educate his only daughter handsomely, present his wife with a fine fur coat—in short, to live, as he put it, like a lord.

A. J. CRONIN:
Shannon's Way (Gollancz, 1948)

135

*THE TRIAL OF WILLIAM JOYCE****

The strong electric light was merciless to William Joyce, whose appearance was a surprise to all of us who knew him only on the air. His voice had suggested a large and flashy handsomeness. But he was a tiny little creature and, though not very ugly, was exhaustively so. His hair was mouse-coloured and grew thinly, particularly above his ears. His nose was joined to his face at an odd angle, and its bridge and its point and its nostrils were all separately misshapen. Above his small dark-blue eyes, which were hard and shiny, like pebbles, his eyebrows were thick and pale and irregular. His neck was long and his shoulders were narrow and sloping. His arms were very short and very thick, so that his sleeves were like little bolsters. His body looked flimsy yet coarse. There was nothing individual about him except a deep scar running across his right cheek from his ear to the corner of his mouth. But this did not create the savage and marred distinction that it might suggest, for it gave a mincing immobility to his mouth, which was extremely small. His smile was pinched and governessy. He was dressed with an intent and ambitious spruceness which did not succeed in giving any impression of well-being, but rather recalled some Eastern European peasant, newly driven off the land by poverty into a factory town and wearing his first suit of Western clothes. He moved with a jerky formality which would have been thought strange in any society. When he bowed to the judge, his bow seemed sincerely respectful but entirely inappropriate to the occasion, and it was difficult to think of any occasion to which it would have been appropriate.

REBECCA WEST:

The Meaning of Treason (Macmillan, 1952)

136

*MR KNOW-ALL**

I did not like Mr Kelada.

I not only shared a cabin with him and ate three meals a day at the same table, but I could not walk round the deck without[1] his joining me. It was impossible to snub him. It never occurred to him that he was not wanted. He was certain that you were as glad to see him as he was to see you. In your own house you might have kicked him downstairs and slammed the door in his face without the suspicion dawning on him that he was not a welcome visitor. He was a good mixer, and in three days knew everyone on board. He ran everything. He managed the sweeps, conducted the auctions, collected money for prizes at the sports, got up quoit and golf matches, organised the concert and arranged the fancy dress ball. He was everywhere and always. He was certainly the best-hated man in the ship. We called him Mr Know-All, even to his face. He took it as a compliment. But it was at meal times that he was most intolerable. For the better part of an hour then he had us at his mercy. He was hearty, jovial, loquacious and argumentative. He knew everything better than anybody else, and it was an affront to his overweening vanity that you should disagree with him. He would not drop a subject, however[2] unimportant, till he had brought you round to his way of thinking. The possibility[3] that he could be mistaken never occurred[4] to him. He was the chap who knew.

W. SOMERSET MAUGHAM:

"Mr Know-All" from *The Complete Short Stories of W. Somerset Maugham* (Vol. 1) (Heinemann, 1951)

[1] § 387. [2] § 253. 2. *Note.* [3] § 373. [4] § 71. 1. *Note*; 4.

137

*A DISTINGUISHED FRENCH PRIEST****

It may be that the French character is today to be seen at its best, not in the literary men, the politicians and the antiquated generals about whom we mostly hear, but in persons who have been lucky enough not to share in the decay of France, who have had some overmastering interest that kept them out of the country or sustained them through the years of demoralisation. One felt, in reading *The Silent World*, by the deep-sea diver Cousteau, that here, rather unexpectedly, was to be seen something of true French greatness: good sense combined with daring, the capacity under all conditions—in this case, the resistance to inhuman pressures, breathing from a tank at the bottom of the sea—for realistic and accurate observation, for exercising a cool intelligence. Such figures, it seems to me, are more satisfactory than most of the people one reads about in say, André Gide's journal, or even than Gide himself. I had of Père de Vaux, in his different department, an impression somewhat similar: intellect, expertness, fortitude, tenacity, an element of daring and—what now seems so rare in France—effectiveness. He has brown eyes of the high-powered headlight kind that seem magnified by his glasses' thick lenses, and long white regular teeth that are always displayed in talking. His sharp nose is of a salience and aquilinity that strongly suggest the Old Testament, as does his coarse bristling brown beard. With his belted white-flannel Dominican robe, the hood of which falls back on his shoulders and at the belt of which hang his beads, he wears a beret, heavy shoes and what look like substantial blue golf stockings. He tells stories extremely well, continually smokes cigarettes and altogether has style, even dash.

EDMUND WILSON:
The Scrolls from the Dead Sea (W. H. Allen, 1955)

138

*WHAT'S IN A NAME?****

He had a wife, too. The Head had been guided by his wife for as long as he could remember, and by his mother before that. He had become Head of his Department in an unusual way. His field was Cowper. Scholars are sown over their fields almost at random, but after a time they begin to resemble what they inhabit, and it all seems to the newcomer Design. But the Head had resembled his field from the beginning; he would have remained in it, as a lump of sugar remains in a cup of tea, except for one thing.

When you pronounce Cowper properly, you say Cooper. People who read about the Head knew that he was an authority on Cowper; if a Frenchman at the University of Manchester had died, he[1] would have been the authority on Cowper. But when people who didn't know how to pronounce Cowper heard the Head referred to by people who did—in speeches, or in conversation, or during the interchanges of professional information that are called by scholars conversation—*they*[2] thought him an authority on Cooper, and spoke of him as such. The Head—he was only a professor[3] in those days—did what he could, but there was not enough that he could do. He explained, but most of the world wasn't there to be explained to; people cared little for Cooper, but less for Cowper—deep down inside, they would *rather* have had him an authority on Cooper: so that advertisements of textbooks of American literature, anthologies of frontier humour, reproductions of Currier and Ives were always there in his pigeonhole in the English office, there in the mail-slot at his office, there in the mail-box on his front porch—people were always stopping him on the campus and asking him Colonial questions, frontier questions, saying to him with a smile, "As an authority on

Cooper you'll be interested in this man Winters: he says Cooper is one of the greatest novelists in English."

RANDALL JARRELL:

Pictures from an Institution (Faber and Faber, 1954)

[1] Avoid the ambiguity of the English. [2] § **234**. 2.
[3] Teaching grade in American universities, roughly equivalent to that of Lecturer in England.

139

*DE GAULLE IN 1940****

For relief I turned to de Gaulle, whose bearing alone among his compatriots matched the calm, healthy phlegm of the British. A strange-looking man, enormously tall; sitting at the table he dominated everyone else by his height, as he had done when walking into the room. No chin, a long, drooping, elephantine nose over a closely-cut moustache, a shadow over a small mouth whose thick lips tended to protrude as if in a pout before speaking, a high, receding forehead and pointed head surmounted by sparse black hair lying flat and neatly parted. His heavily-hooded eyes were very shrewd. When about to speak he oscillated his head slightly, like a pendulum, while searching for words. I at once remembered and understood the nickname of "*Le Connétable*" which Pétain said had been given him at St Cyr. It was easy to imagine that head on a ruff, that secret face at Catherine de Medici's Council Chamber.

I studied him with great interest, little thinking that for a while we should both be bent with such complete concentration on the same task, nor that later we should be driven so far apart.

That afternoon he had a look of confidence and self-possession which was very appealing. He had, I thought, brought it from Abbeville, where he had fought a successful tank action (the only one). Fresh air had given his sallow skin a healthy colour. His cheeks were almost pink. That freshness of complexion I never saw on his face again, nor, I think, did I often see him smile as he did when he turned towards me then. It was a frank, confident smile that belied his usual expression and made me feel I should greatly like this man. I perceived that afternoon what was perhaps the real de Gaulle, or maybe that part of him which might have prevailed had he remained a soldier, straight, direct, even rather brutal.

Sir Edward Spears:
"The Fall of France" (*Assignment to Catastrophe*, Vol. II) (Heinemann, 1954)

REFLECTIVE AND PHILOSOPHICAL

140

*THE LIMITATIONS OF THE SCIENTIST**

If anyone doubts Boyle's Law, then he can restage Boyle's experiments until he is satisfied. If he wishes to be sure of the character of penicillin, he can grow and regrow the mould until he is exhausted. And the processes of mathematical reasoning used in other branches of science are equally copper-bottomed and incapable of misleading. Scientific generalisations are based upon an enormous and often unrealised[1] foundation of detailed investigation; they are overturned (and that[2] rarely) by the piecemeal destruction of that foundation. So, to a[3] scientist, knowledge can easily seem to consist in systematisation; when the information has been co-ordinated and set into a pattern, then you have knowledge, and that knowledge is sure.

But in the outside world, the world of economics, history and politics, the world of human activities in short, there are no exact facts, and no experiment can ever be repeated. All generalisations are vague and inaccurate; they are little more[4] than metaphors. No town is really like another, no class is like another, or even the same as it was ten years before. As for testing by experiment, you cannot even repeat so much as a general election in the same conditions. Good sense and skill in these subjects are founded on a knowledge and estimate of nuances, tendencies, probabilities, ideologies and old history. The scientist, for whom systematisation is truth, is especially disqualified in judging these.

RAYMOND POSTGATE:

The Ledger is Kept (Michael Joseph, 1953)

[1] Does this word mean "whose significance is not understood," or "not brought into existence?" In either case, it is probably more natural to attach it, in the French, to "investigation" (*recherches*).

[2] "that": introduce a phrase by *ce qui*.

[3] Use the definite article.

[4] § **272**.

141

*THE VAGARIES OF MEMORY*****

If indeed we depended solely on a purely spontaneous memory we should be reduced to the barest pittance of the past. But since at every moment of the day our senses and our thoughts revive in us that past--and every perception is largely compounded of recognition—memory *appears* to be all but infinite in its resources. And if we aid the survey of our chosen period with artificial reminders of any kind, our recollection of it, far from being a wilderness, blossoms like the rose—though it may often be a faded rose. Occasional startling breakdowns occur even here—as when two friends, and familiar friends, who are unknown to one another come to see you and, on attempting to introduce them, you fail to recall either's name! A complete bevy of names indeed—of flowers or what not—may be habitually elusive; in my own case, hydrangea, saxifrage, bergamot, cyclamen, gladiolus. The sight of any one of these, almost always evokes a sort of aura where the name should be, and as often as not two or three others of the bevy will politely present themselves instead! Names are merely tags or labels, whatever value we put upon our own; but a failure of this kind, caused probably by some clumsy personal interference in the workings of the mind, had best be forgotten. It is else only too likely to recur. In general, reminders are successful even though moderately so. As Proust discovered by deliberate and ingenious devices—smells and scents, the taste of cake dipped in tea and so forth—there is an immense field of the *revivable* which we seldom make any effort to retrieve. How much of it, and in what proportion that much is to the irrevocable, only the psycho-analyst could declare.

What is needed is a crafty hint, a significant cue, an inviting nucleus. The skein of silk is there, that is certain. We must grope very heedfully for a loose end. The cue must accord in some respect with our need. We must fish with the appropriate fly. The recovery of but a note or two of music, enough to shape an air or melody, may suffice for the wherewithal of a song unheard since infancy. *Sesame!*—it is done. A word or two about a minor character in a novel—say, his long nose, his narrow feet, his hat-band; the briefest hint of some crucial scene or episode—and the 'forgotten' tale itself like a bird's-eye view of a familiar countryside may at once swiftly revive in the mind. Its aura too; what we mean when we say it is a good, or bad, or stupid, or astonishing book.

WALTER DE LA MARE:
Early One Morning (Faber and Faber, 1935)

142

*MODERN PHILOSOPHICAL METHOD****

So, then, the general conception of analysis was that of a kind of translation, or, perhaps better, a kind of paraphrase. For it was to be translation within a language, not from one language to another: a translation from a less explicit to a more explicit form, or from a misleading to an unmisleading form. If your problem was, say, the nature of *truth*, or, say, the nature of *existence*, you hoped to solve it by finding a formula for translating sentences in which the adjective 'true' or the verb 'exists' occurred, into sentences in which these expressions did not occur, and in which no straightforward synonyms of them occurred either. Nor[1] was this, after all, so very revolutionary a conception of philosophy. The search for definitions of problematic ideas was almost as old as philosophy itself. What was new was rather the substitution of sentences for words, of propositions for concepts, as the unit upon which analysis was to be practised. And for this change, as earlier lectures have shown, there were very good reasons.

Although, in Cambridge, Wittgenstein was already doing something very different, on the whole the method of analysis dominated English philosophy in the thirties. It brought some advances in some fields. But in the main the results were disappointing. The sentences of common speech seemed somehow to resist the simplifying expansions which theory had prepared for them. Even Russell's earlier brilliant glosses on the structure of ordinary sentences, in terms of the syntax of the new formal logic, began in the end to seem a little queer. And those who went to work with fewer preconceptions about their results were apt to find that if they preserved the sense of the original, they achieved no simplification: and that if they gained a simplification, they did so at the cost of losing the sense.

P. F. STRAWSON:

"Construction and Analysis" from *The Revolution in Philosophy* (Macmillan, 1956)

[1] § **311**. 1. *Note* 2.

143

*TRAVEL HINTS***

No travel hints would be complete without some word of caution about shipboard romances, engagements and marriages. The girl or young man you fell in love with on the ship when it was in Southern waters and the orchestra was playing "Night and Day" is going to be subjected to a cruel and rigorous test standing there by a gloomy pile of baggage in a bleak and chilly ship shed. If the swan suddenly becomes a goose, or the knight a clodhopper, it is what is known as 'undergoing[1] a land change.' If you were married aboard ship and[2] the bride, or bridegroom, now appeals to you about as much as a piece of cold whole-wheat toast, you are in a rather serious jam. In America you cannot have a marriage annulled on the ground that it was contracted while you were under the influence of the Gulf Stream and Cole Porter. If you are a man, I suggest that you treat your inamorata with a gallantry tempered by caution during the voyage out and back, and refrain[3] from proposing until you have caught her on the dock. If she is going to be met by her mother and father, her Aunt Louise and her Uncle Bert, you will want to get a look at them first too. During the cruise try to engage the girl of your dreams in discussions of books or politics if you find yourself with her on the promenade deck in the moonlight, while the band is playing "I Told Every Little

Star." It won't work, but try it. All this, I suppose, is really no more concern of mine than why you keep fireworks in the house, so I will not pursue it further.

JAMES THURBER:

Thurber Country (Hamish Hamilton, 1953)

[1] § **90** (*b*). [2] § **388**. (*'If' clauses.*)
[3] "refrain" needs the same construction as "treat."

144

*PERCEPTION AND REALITY*****

The common world in which we believe ourselves to live is a construction, partly scientific, partly pre-scientific. We perceive tables as circular or rectangular, in spite of the fact that a painter, to reproduce their appearance, has to paint ellipses or non-rectangular quadrilaterals. We see a person as of about the same size whether he is two feet from us or twelve. Until our attention is drawn to the facts, we are quite unconscious of the corrections that experience has led us to make in interpreting sensible appearances. There is a long journey from the child who draws two eyes in a profile to the physicist who talks of electrons and protons, but throughout this journey there is one constant purpose: to eliminate the subjectivity of sensation, and substitute a kind of knowledge which can be the same for all percipients. Gradually the difference between what is sensed and what is believed to be objective grows greater; the child's profile with two eyes is still very like what is seen, but the electrons and protons have only a remote resemblance of logical structure. The electrons and protons, however, have the merit that they *may* be what actually exists where there are no sense-organs, whereas our immediate visual data, owing to their subjectivity, are almost certainly not what takes place in the physical objects that we are said to see.

The electrons and protons—assuming it scientifically correct to believe in them—do not depend for their existence upon being perceived; on the contrary, there is every reason to believe that they existed for countless ages before there were any percipients in the universe. But although perception is not needed to give us a reason for their existence, it is needed to give us a reason for believing in their existence. Hundreds of thousands of years ago, a vast and remote region emitted incredible numbers of photons, which wandered through the universe in all directions. At last a very few of them hit a photographic plate, in which they caused chemical changes which made parts of the plate look black instead of white when examined by an astronomer. This tiny effect upon a minute but highly educated organism is our only reason for believing in the existence of a nebula comparable in size with the Milky Way.

BERTRAND RUSSELL:

Human Knowledge, its Scope and Limits (Allen and Unwin, 1948)

145

*ON GROWING OLDER****

Children commonly wish to be taken for a little older than they really are because they associate the progress of the years with the graduated acquisition of extra privileges. Responsibilities and cares, loaded on the back along with the privileges, are hardly felt till the weight of them settles into place. Adolescents desire to pass as adult because of impatience and the urges of emulation. And so begins a life-long process of incomplete adjustment to the outer world. The young man and woman may glory in their new-found combination of youth, maturity, and independence, yet they are always noting, with a mixture of jealousy and humility, the superior *savoir-faire* of those in the thirties, and will be flattered if they are admitted on equal terms to the counsels of their elders. Then there comes a time when they are best pleased if opinion credits them with more wisdom and experience than their years and—simultaneously—with looking younger than they really are. This is the topmost ridge of their careers. After this they have done with imitating the behaviour of their elders, and a new younger generation, thrusting upward, is all too ready to point out that the bloom is off their youth. Flattery can reach them only by imputing freshness to their appearance. And so for the second half of adult life each of us lives behind a mask which, he feels, belies the truth: our faces look wiser and more staid than we know we are. We can get along very well with our contemporaries, crack our little jokes, play the fool when the mood is on us, kick up our mental heels. Those who are of an age with us understand: they have perforce to be tolerant, knowing that behind their own ageing faces the spirit is still impenitently youthful. But in the presence of our juniors we must behave more decorously. If they respect us it shows they acknowledge our superior experience, of which we are, illogically, just as proud as of our mental sprightliness: lest we sink in their opinion, and conduct ourselves ridiculously like sheep gambolling among the lambs, we respond to the expectation of our juniors: we become outwardly grave and reverend. And if they fail to show the respect due to us we turn severe: we visit them with our displeasure; for, behind our matured faces, we are still touchy with the vanity of youth.

JOHN BROPHY:
The Human Face (Harrap, 1945)

146

*IDIOSYNCRASIES IN PARENTS***

I was absurdly critical of certain little peculiarities of my parents which today I not only regard with affectionate amusement, but actually find myself repeating in some similar form.

My father, given the opportunity, would bare his body to the sun. Of course this was eminently sensible, and in accord with his own views and the latest teachings of his day and age in preventive medicine. Yet as an adolescent I used privately to regard it[1] as ridiculous and embarrassing for[1] a middle-aged man to stride along the seashore in shorts, reciting Shakespeare with a Panama hat protecting his bald head. Perhaps[2] there is a simple Freudian explanation. However, now I find myself, whether it is on the shores of the Pacific, the Atlantic, the Mediterranean or at Margate during a Labour Party conference, stealing away to the sea to bathe or, as a second-best, to paddle, and perhaps to declaim to the ocean when well out of earshot of the beach. Perhaps you have noticed this!

Of course these are minor idiosyncrasies of which one is well aware. Unfortunately, those traits which heredity, environment and education have combined to implant in one are not readily recognised and therefore the unfortunate parent—unless he or she is addicted to some major vice—is unaware of what irritates or even alienates the child.

For these reasons I am not surprised to hear that family relationships are discussed freely in your little circle at Oxford. You will certainly hear[3] more views expressed on the subject than you did at school.

The schoolgirl is apt to accept the family behaviour pattern without much criticism and her school friends become merged with her family life. It is when she arrives at her 'teens and becomes keenly aware of the world outside her home that she begins to question and analyse the family circle and its relations one to the other.

DR EDITH SUMMERSKILL:
Letters to my Daughter (Heinemann, 1957)

[1] *Cf.* § **223**. 2. [2] § **344**. 1. [3] § **229**.

147

*SPECULATIONS ON GOODNESS*****

We have now seen reason to reject three major types of theory of the nature of personal goodness, or virtue. The first sought to derive it from the agent's conscientiousness; that is, from his direct moral judgments: the second interpreted it according to our own removed judgments of moral rightness or wrongness: the third sought to equate it with a sum of the agent's specific virtues. It is now necessary to offer a positive account of its meaning which will do justice to the following facts: first, that the conscientious man is considered to be virtuous; second, that there is a tendency on our part (although it is not fully jnstified) to believe that the man whose actions appear to be morally right is a virtuous man; third, that there is a connection between virtue and the possession of specific virtues.

It will be possible to avoid some of the confusions into which the analysis of virtue has fallen if we make clear that the term 'virtue' does not in fact refer to what we have been calling a character-attribute: it is not, properly speaking, a *part* of a person's character at all. Instead, it is a quality predicated of that character; the quality of being wholly good or, in the case of vice, of being morally bad. Whenever we predicate goodness or badness of an entity we regard these qualities as truly descriptive of that entity, but (in Ross's terminology) we do not regard them as constitutive ('natural') parts. So it is here. To speak of a person as virtuous or vicious, as good or evil, as noble or corrupt, is to predicate moral value or disvalue of that person's character as a whole; it is not to assign a specific character-attribute to him.

MAURICE MANDELBAUM:

The Phenomenology of Moral Experience (The Free Press of Glencoe, Illinois, 1955)

148

*RIVER SOURCES**

When I consider the sources of rivers which I have seen, there is not one, I think, which I do not remember to have had[1] about it an influence of awe. Not only because one could in imagination see the kingdoms or the cities which it was to visit and the way in which it would bind them all together in one province and one story, but also simply because it was an origin.

The sources of the Rhone are famous: the Rhone comes out of a glacier through a sort of ice cave, and if it were not for an enormous hotel quite four-square it would be as lonely a place as there is in Europe, and as remarkable a beginning for a great river as could anywhere be found. Nor,[2] when you come to think of it, does any European river have such varied fortunes as the Rhone. It feeds such different religions and looks on such diverse landscapes. It makes Geneva and it makes Avignon; it changes in colour and in the nature of its going as it goes. It sees new products appearing continually on its journey until[3] it comes to olives, and it flows past the beginning of human cities, when it reflects the huddle of old Arles.

The sources of the Garonne are well known. The Garonne rises by itself in a valley from which there is no issue, like the fabled valleys shut in by hills on every side. And if it were anything but the Garonne it would not be able to escape: it would lie imprisoned there for ever. Being the Garonne it tunnels a way for itself right under the High Pyrenees and comes out again on the French side. There are some that doubt this, but then there are people who would doubt anything.

HILAIRE BELLOC:

First and Last (Methuen, 1911)

[1] "I do not remember having seen one which did not," etc.
[2] § **311**. 2. [3] § **385**.

149

*INNER SENSE*****

Philosophy is employed on objects of the *inner* SENSE, and cannot, like geometry, appropriate to every construction a correspondent *outward* intuition. Nevertheless, philosophy, if it is to arrive at evidence, must proceed from the most original construction, and the question then is, what is the most original construction or first productive act for the inner sense. The answer to this question depends on the direction which is given to the inner sense. But in philosophy the inner sense cannot have its direction determined by an outward object. To the original construction of the line I can be compelled by a line drawn before me on the slate or on sand. The stroke thus drawn is indeed not the line itself, but only the image or picture of the line. It is not from it, that we first learn to know the line; but, on the contrary, we bring this stroke to the original line generated by the act of the imagination; otherwise we could not define it as without breadth or thickness. Still however this stroke is the sensuous image of the original or ideal line, and an efficient mean to excite *every* imagination to the intuition of it.

It is demanded then, whether there be found any means in philosophy to determine the direction of the inner sense, as in mathematics it is determinable by its specific image or outward picture. Now the inner sense has its direction determined for the greater part only by an act of freedom. One man's consciousness extends only to the pleasant or unpleasant sensations caused in him by external impressions; another enlarges his inner sense to a consciousness of forms and quantity; a third in addition to the image is conscious of the conception or notion of the thing; a fourth attains to a notion of his notions—he reflects on his own reflections; and thus we may say without impropriety, that the one possesses more or less inner sense, than the other. This more or less betrays already, that philosophy in its first principles must have a practical or moral, as well as a theoretical or speculative side. This difference in degree does not exist in the mathematics.

S. T. COLERIDGE:
Biographia Literaria

150

*THE OUTSIDER****

For the Outsider, the world into which he has been born is always a world without values. Compared to his own appetite for a purpose and a direction, the way most men live is not living at all; it is drifting. This is the Outsider's wretchedness, for all men have a herd instinct that leads them to believe that what the majority does must be right. Unless he can evolve a set of values that will correspond to his own higher intensity of purpose, he may as well throw himself under a bus, for he will always be an outcast and a misfit.

But once this purpose is found, the difficulties are half over. Let the Outsider accept without further hesitation: I am different from other men because I have been destined to something greater; let him see himself in the role of predestined prophet or world-betterer, and a half of the Outsider's problems have been solved. What he is saying is, in effect, this: In most men, the instinct of brotherhood with other men is stronger—the herd instinct; in *me*, a sense of brotherhood with something other than man is strongest, and demands priority. When the Outsider comes to look at other men closely and sympathetically, the hard and fast distinctions break down; he cannot say: I am a poet and they are not, for he soon comes to recognise that no one is entirely a businessman, just as no poet is entirely a poet. He can only say: the sense of purpose that makes me a poet is stronger than theirs. His needle swings to magnetic pole without hesitation; theirs wavers around all the points of the compass and only points north when they come particularly close to the pole, when under the influence of drink or patriotism or sentimentality. I speak of these last three conditions without disparagement; all forms of stimulation of man's sense of purpose are equally valid and, if applied for long enough, would have the effect of making a man into an Outsider.

COLIN WILSON:

The Outsider (Gollancz, 1956)

151

*THE REVOLUTION IN PHYSICS*****

But in our century it is just in this sphere that fundamental changes have taken place in the basis of atomic physics which have made us abandon the world-view of ancient atomic philosophy. It has become clear that the desired objective reality of the elementary particles is too crude an over-simplification of what really happens, and that it must give way to very much more abstract conceptions. For if we wish to form a picture of the nature of these elementary particles, we can no longer ignore the physical processes through which we obtain our knowledge of them. While, in observing everyday objects, the physical process involved in making the observation plays a subsidiary role only, in the case of the smallest building particles of matter, every process of observation produces a large disturbance. We can no longer speak of the behaviour of the particle independently of the process of observation. As a final consequence, the natural laws formulated mathematically in quantum theory no longer deal with the elementary particles themselves but with our knowledge of them. Nor is it any longer possible to ask whether or not these particles exist in space and time objectively, since the only processes we can refer to as taking place are those which represent the interplay of particles with some other physical system, *e.g.*, a measuring instrument.

Thus, the objective reality of the elementary particles has been strangely dispersed, not into the fog of some new ill-defined or still unexplained conception of reality, but into the transparent clarity of a mathematics that no longer describes the behaviour of the elementary particles but only our knowledge of this behaviour. The atomic physicist has had to resign himself to the fact that his science is but a link in the infinite chain of man's argument with nature, *and that it cannot simply speak of nature 'in itself.'* Science always presupposes the existence of man and, as Bohr has said, we must become conscious of the fact that we are not merely observers but also actors on the stage of life.

WERNER HEISENBERG:
The Physicist's Conception of Nature (Hutchinson, 1958)

152

*LONGEVITY****

But of course what the critics wrote about Edward Driffield was eye-wash. His outstanding merit was not the realism that gave vigour to his work, nor the beauty that informed it, nor his graphic portraits of seafaring men, nor his poetic descriptions of salty marshes, of storm and calm, and of nestling hamlets; it was his longevity. Reverence for old age is one of the most admirable traits of the human race, and I think it may safely be stated that in no other country than ours is[1] this trait more marked. The awe and love with which other nations regard old age is often platonic; but ours is practical. Who but the English would fill Covent Garden to listen to an aged *prima donna* without a voice? Who but the English would pay to see dancers so decrepit that they can hardly put one foot before the other and say to one another admiringly in the intervals: "By George, sir, d'you know he's a long way past sixty?" But compared with politicians and writers these are but striplings, and I often think that a *jeune premier* must be of a singularly amiable disposition if it does not make him bitter to consider that when at the age of seventy he must end his career the public man and the author are only at their prime. A man who is a politician at forty is a statesman at three score and ten. It is at this age, when he would be too old to be a clerk or a gardener or a police-court magistrate, that he is ripe to govern a country. This is not so strange when you reflect that from the earliest times the old have rubbed it into the young that they are wiser than they, and before the young have discovered what nonsense this was they were old too, and it profited them to carry on the imposture; and besides, no one can have moved in the society of politicians without discovering that (if one may judge by results) it requires little mental ability to rule a nation. But why writers should be more esteemed the older they grow, has long perplexed me.

W. Somerset Maugham:

Cakes and Ale (Heinemann, 1930)

[1] Can the inversion be maintained in the French?

153

*THE INSUFFICIENCY OF REASON*****

What intellectual people find so hard to get into their heads is the complete helplessness of human reason in the presence of the mystery of the world. Our reason is adapted with proud and lively exactitude, as Bergson so admirably pointed out, to the crudest, lowest, and most unimportant aspects of the Dimension which hems us in.

It is completely blocked in its approach to the reality of things by the obtruding presences of Time and Space, who like a pair of monstrous Punchinellos—one striking on the gong of a clock whose echoes refuse to cease, the other emptying starry marbles out of a pocket that seems bottomless—so deafen and dazzle it that it takes electrons for living affections, mathematical symbols for living persons, and the extremely limited dimension that surrounds us for the Totality of Being.

Not on any ground at all has the human race the right to arrogate to itself a position so superior to the other creatures of the earth that while they must perish at death it alone survives. All that lives in this Dimension, and this includes the whole chemical mass of the so-called Inanimate, has a portion of its identity in the next Dimension. In this Dimension there is a perpetual process of birth, growth, decline, and death.

Nor are any entities, from the most active and sentient to the most immobile and insentient, exempt from the law under which we come into existence, live out our allotted span, and fall, easily or painfully, under the common doom.

This is all that reason can tell us. Life-death, death-life, life-death, in an inexhaustible and inescapable alternation! But reason is not the most subtle, nor by any means the most comprehensive organ of research we possess. Reason is easily drugged and bound and tossed into their car by the marauding gangsters, Time and Space.

And not only so! Reason is always, even when left to herself, *a little mad*. Not mad in a noble, reckless, heroic way, but mad in cold, deliberate, mean, concentrated, fanatic ruthlessness, like inquisitors and vivisectors!

JOHN COWPER POWYS:
Mortal Strife (Jonathan Cape, 1942)

154

*DEALING WITH LITTER****

Life is one long struggle to disinter oneself, to keep one's head above the accumulations, the ever-deepening layers of objects, of litter (for so I call those objects which I do not want), which attempt to cover one over, steadily, almost irresistibly, like falling snow. The danger is (one has heard) that one is lulled to sleep beneath the drifts, and will not (so also one has heard) wake again, but lie for ever besnowed, buried, unable to stir. Courage, then: fight the insidious, the deadly drifts while there is yet time; up and scatter them to the winds, tear them to shreds, fling them into dustbins, into the street, anywhere, and stand up free and disencumbered to abide the next storms.

If one had the wisdom to cast out litter as it arrives each day, one would not have these mighty periodic disencumberments; one would live more easily; but one would miss that tremendous, that spacious, sense of easement which follows a great clearance.

Tear them up, then, those piles of letters which you have never answered, nor will. Are you not born free? Shall[1] anyone with a pen or a typewriter, a stamp or two, and some stationery, have the power to assault you, to bully you, to tear your precious time and your frail brain and attention, so sorely needed elsewhere, to shreds by making you answer his letters? You do not, I am sure, write to all and sundry asking them this and that, requesting them for time, for gifts, for attention to some business in which you, but not they, may chance to be interested: you give them credit for having their own interests, their own work, their own lives and schemes. You let them, in fact (I hope), alone. But how unusual this abstention appears to be! Letters arrive for you; pamphlets, newspaper cuttings, books, discursive remarks, all manner of suggestions and requests. There they lie, reproachful piles, awaiting your attention.

ROSE MACAULAY:

Personal Pleasures (Gollancz, 1935)

[1] "Shall" is used here with full meaning. See § **94**. 2.

155

*THE ALLEGORY OF WINTER*****

Ought not winter, in allegorical designs, the rather to be represented with such things that might suggest hope than such as convey a cold and grim despair? The withered leaf, the snowflake, the hedging bill that cuts and destroys, why these? Why not rather the dear larks for one? They fly in flocks, and amid the white expanse of snow (in the south) their pleasant twitter or call is heard as they sweep along seeking some grassy spot cleared by the wind. The lark, the bird of the light, is there in the bitter short days. Put the lark then for winter, a sign of hope, a certainty of summer. Put, too, the sheathed bud, for if you search the hedge you will find the buds there, on tree and bush, carefully wrapped around with the case which protects them as a cloak. Put, too, the sharp needles of the green corn; let the wind clear it of snow a little way, and show that under cold clod and colder snow the green thing pushes up, knowing that summer must come. Nothing despairs but man. Set the sharp curve of the white new moon in the sky; she is white in true frost, and yellow a little if it is devising change. Set the new moon as something that symbols an increase. Set the shepherd's crook in a corner as a token that the flocks are already enlarged in number. The shepherd is the symbolic man of the hardest winter time. His work is never more important than then. Those that only roam the fields when they are pleasant in May, see the lambs at play in the meadow, and naturally think of lambs and May flowers. But the lamb was born in the adversity of snow. Or you might set the morning star, for it burns and burns and glitters in the winter dawn, and throws forth beams like those of metal consumed in oxygen. There is nought that I know by comparison with which I might indicate the glory of the morning star, while yet the dark night hides in the hollows. The lamb is born in the fold. The morning star glitters in the sky. The bud is alive in its sheath; the green corn under the snow; the lark twitters as he passes. Now these to me are the allegory of winter.

RICHARD JEFFERIES:
The Open Air

156

*SPIRITUAL CONCENTRATION****

At this point it is worth remarking parenthetically that God is by no means the only possible object of contemplation. There have been and still are many philosophic, aesthetic and scientific contemplatives. One-pointed concentration on that which is not the highest may become a dangerous form of idolatry. In a letter to Hooker, Darwin wrote that "it is a cursed evil to any man to become so absorbed in any subject as I am in mine." It is an evil because such one-pointedness may result in the more or less total atrophy of all but one side of the mind. Darwin himself records that in later life he was unable to take the smallest interest in poetry, art or religion. Professionally, in relation to his chosen specialty, a man may be completely mature. Spiritually and sometimes even ethically, in relation to God and his neighbours, he may be hardly more than a foetus.

In cases where the one-pointed contemplation is of God there is also a risk that the mind's unemployed capacities may atrophy. The hermits of Tibet and the Thebaïd were certainly one-pointed, but with a one-pointedness of exclusion and mutilation. It may be, however, that if they had been more truly 'docile to the Holy Ghost,' they would have come to understand that the one-pointedness of exclusion is at best a preparation for the one-pointedness of inclusion—the realisation of God in the fullness of cosmic being as well as in the interior height of the individual soul. Like the Taoist sage, they would at last have turned back into the world riding on their tamed and regenerate individuality; they would have 'come eating and drinking,' would have associated with 'publicans and sinners' or their Buddhist equivalents, 'wine-bibbers and butchers.'

ALDOUS HUXLEY:

The Perennial Philosophy (Chatto and Windus, 1946)

157

*WORK AND LEISURE**

The function of the machine is to save work. In a fully mechanised world all the dull drudgery will be done by machinery, leaving us free for[1] more interesting pursuits. So expressed, this sounds splendid. It makes one[2] sick to see half a dozen men sweating their guts out to dig a trench for[1] a water-pipe, when some easily[3] devised machine would scoop the earth out in a couple of minutes. Why not let the machine do the work and the men go and do something else. But presently the question arises, what else are they to do? Supposedly they are set free from 'work' in order that[4] they may do something which is not 'work.' But what is work and what is not work? Is it work to[5] dig, to carpenter, to plant trees, to fell trees, to ride, to fish, to hunt, to feed chickens, to play the piano, to take photographs, to build a house, to cook, to sew, to trim hats, to mend motor bicycles? All of these things are work to somebody, and all of them are play to somebody. There are in fact very few activities which cannot be classed either as work or play according as you choose to regard them. The labourer set free from digging may want to spend his leisure, or part of it, in playing the piano, while the professional pianist may be only too glad to get out and dig at the potato patch. Hence the antithesis between work, as something intolerably tedious and not-work, as something desirable, is false.

GEORGE ORWELL:
The Road to Wigan Pier (Gollancz, 1937)

[1] "for": use a verbal construction. [2] § **241. 2.**
[3] Use *facile* with an adverbial infinitive. § **101.** [4] § **385.** [5] § **110.**

158

*ON IDLENESS*****

There is nothing more common among this torpid generation than murmurs and complaints; murmurs at uneasiness which only vacancy and suspicion expose them to feel, and complaints of distresses which it is in their power to remove. Laziness is commonly associated with timidity. Either fear originally prohibits endeavours by infusing despair of success; or the frequent failure of irresolute struggles, and the constant desire of avoiding labour, impress by degrees false terrors on the mind. But fear, whether natural or acquired, when once it has full possession of the fancy, never fails to employ it upon visions of calamity, such as, if they are not dissipated by useful employment, will soon overcast it with horrors, and embitter life not only with those miseries by which all earthly beings are really more or less tormented, but with those which do not yet exist, and which can only be discerned by the perspicacity of cowardice.

Among all who sacrifice future advantage to present inclination, scarcely any gain so little as those that suffer themselves to freeze in idleness. Others are corrupted by some enjoyment of more or less power to gratify the passions; but to neglect our duties, merely to avoid the labour of performing them, a labour which is always punctually rewarded, is surely to sink under weak temptations. Idleness never can secure tranquillity; the call of reason and of conscience will pierce the closest pavilion of the sluggard; and though it may not have force to drive him from his down, will be loud enough to hinder him from sleep. Those moments which he cannot resolve to make useful by devoting them to the great business of his being, will still be usurped by powers that will not leave them to his disposal; remorse and vexation will seize upon them, and forbid him to enjoy what he is so desirous to appropriate.

SAMUEL JOHNSON:

From *The Rambler* of 29th June, 1751

159

*VISUALISING ATOMIC STRUCTURES*****

What is it to supply a theory? It is to offer an intelligible, systematic, conceptual pattern for the observed data. The value of this pattern lies in its capacity to unite phenomena which, without the theory, are either surprising, anomalous, or wholly unnoticed. Democritus' atomic theory avoids investing atoms with those secondary properties requiring explanation. It provides a pattern of concepts whereby the properties the atom *does* possess—position, shape, motion—can, as a matter of course, account for the other 'secondary' properties of objects. The price paid for this intellectual gain is unpicturability.

Atomic explanation did not change; scholars remained unable to visualise atoms, just as Democritus' contemporaries had been. As the theory gained support in chemistry and physics, however, scientists came to regard atoms as familiar things. When speaking strictly they renounced the picturable atom; but why speak so strictly? The geometer never denies himself the use of drawn lines: lines *should* be one-dimensional, but proofs and constructions cannot be carried out with one-dimensional lines. Similarly, physicists could think about atoms only by visualising them. Why not? It helped to secure explanations. Thus the almost invisible diagrams of geometry crept into physical thinking about atoms. Rutherford was thinking on these lines in 1911 when he accepted Nagaoka's idea "of a 'Saturnian' atom which . . . consist(s) of a central attracting mass surrounded by rings of rotating electrons." Atoms should have been as unpicturable as the entities of geometry, but no physicist chose so to paralyse his thinking. Indeed, atoms became models of geometrical and dynamical behaviour, and this made them eminently picturable. Why should colours and lines be more than a practical necessity? Like ideal circles, the classical atom was just the limit of a series of sketches of increasing fineness.

Even this expedient no longer serves the imagination. Atomic explanation always ruled out secondary qualities; now modern atomic explanation denies its fundamental units any direct correspondence with the primary qualities, the traditional dimensions, positions, and dynamical properties. In classical physics kinematical studies precede dynamical ones; in quantum physics this division and order is not feasible.

N. R. HANSON:

Patterns of Discovery (Cambridge University Press, 1958)

MISCELLANEOUS PASSAGES DEALING WITH MODERN LIFE AND THOUGHT

160

*DO IT YOURSELF**

The jobs we Do Ourselves never seem to be clear-cut, creative projects like laying carpets or making bookcases. They are sprawling, inconclusive jobs: *defence* works against the ceaseless advance of decay and ruin: part of the endless fight to stop England from reverting, first to a waste land covered with purple flowers, then right back[1] to a damp Temperate Forest. We have to keep the frogs out.

The other night I had just replaced a leaky washer in the kitchen (I can Do *That* Myself) when I found that water had been dribbling down for weeks inside the squalid cupboard under the sink; and it had spread underneath a large corner of our beautiful new black linoleum.

Well, there are no Handy Kits for drying linoleum—the *underside of linoleum*, the canvassy stuff. My plan[2] was to turn it back and point an electric fire at the affected part. But you can't point an electric fire downwards: it's on the floor already. We don't keep an electric fire in the kitchen. I brought one from upstairs:[3] I suspended it from the curtain rail with string, so that it pointed down at the linoleum from a height of 3 ft (and it's astonishing how often you can trip over turned-up linoleum even when you have just turned it up yourself). I had an urgent feeling that I was just in time to dry out this linoleum, that if I left it another day it would rot. Supper was ready. The only power-point was for the washing machine. It took a different kind of plug from the one on the fire.

PAUL JENNINGS:
Gladly Oddly (Max Reinhardt, 1958)

[1] Translate by an adjective attached to "forest," *e.g.*, *primordial(e)*.
[2] Use a verb in the first person. [3] § **63**. 2. *Note.*

161

*A MAN'S WORLD?***

Why, for instance, is it a foregone conclusion[1] that time-tables are[2] something 'for men only' and that it is unmanly or un-gallant or un-something to stand by and allow a woman to look up a train? This might not be tiresome if the man wouldn't always adopt the attitude that the woman isn't quite bright. I pride myself on being rather expert at reading time-tables. I can tell at a glance whether you read them down or up and I even understand those archaeological little signs that indicate whether the train carries a diner or a 'buffet-lounge,' but I'm never permitted to prove it. Start opening a time-table in the presence of a gent and again that 'Allow-me-Madam' spirit comes upon him. He grabs the sheet from your hand, losing the correct place you've already found, and starts groping either among the pages of 'stations listed in this folder' or the pictures of Nature's Beauty Spots in the back. In my case the situation is further complicated by the fact that most of my gallants have reached the time of life when not only do they grab for the time-table, they have also to grab for their glasses. And all the while they're adjusting these with one hand and making a mess of the time-table with the other, one must stand by and look grateful and fragile and dumb. It's very trying.

The same thing applies to road-maps and to names in the telephone book. The average woman is just as speedy as the average man at finding what she's looking for in the 'phone directory, but it would be a bitter blow to masculine pride to let it be known.

CORNELIA OTIS SKINNER:
That's Me All Over (Constable, 1949)

[1] Turn by a verb + adverbial phrase. [2] § 373.

162

*A WOMAN'S WORLD?***

Today there is a wider choice of careers for women. They are also earning more in real terms than they did in similar jobs before the war. The domestication of men, another effect of the war, and the current wave of do-it-yourself has made husbands more personally involved with the gadgets and comforts provided in their homes. Considerable sums are spent on home maintenance and improvement; the amount set aside from wages for the household has increased, and so has the wife's status as organiser of the home. Today 85 per cent of spending is done by women.

Thanks to hire-purchase, the standards continually being urged upon one and all by television and through the mass media are those of middle-class origin—the family car, the washing machine, the refrigerator, the occasional holiday abroad. Habits of dress no longer indicate reliably the wearer's social class or outlook. Before the war, for example, no woman's weekly would have touched the model girl who appeared in *Vogue*. The cold, leisured, moneyed look would have alienated the average reader. Nowadays, with fashion wearing a natural air—"They all look," said one editress, "as if they never combed their hair"—the same girl can model a mink or a cotton print.[1] The woman's magazines, whose fictional heroes and heroines have always tended to have vaguely middle-class occupations—doctors, journalists, advertising men, barristers, and now archaeologists, have simply swum with the stream. And women who, on the whole, are more conscious of social differences and attitudes than men, have accepted the scale of values prescribed by the magazines and have trusted them as the arbiters of what is 'right' in the race to keep up.

SUSAN HICKLIN:

"Strictly for Women" from *Progress*, the magazine of the Unilever Group

[1] "a mink or a cotton print": *i.e.* "a mink coat or a cotton print dress."

163

*A VISIT FROM A TELEVISION UNIT****

The whole house was by now disguised as a studio. Cables snaked about the floor in almost every room. Lights and cameras and microphones were set up and taken down. Children, visitors, animals and dailies tripped over wires, knocked over instruments and generally entangled themselves in it all. My mother, who happened to call, looked upon televising as a childish game that could be tolerated for a short time but should not be allowed to interfere with the straightforward business of getting on with things. She started to tidy the house for me, several times unconsciously crossing a whirring camera in front of a child or animal that the team had spent hours on trying to arrange for a natural-looking shot.

The idea was to film the children doing ordinary things in an ordinary way. They were taken eating, washing their hands, going up and down stairs, drawing, sewing, playing the piano, acting in the attic theatre, getting in and out of the van, and feeding the hens. But gradually, as their enthusiasm for the limelight began to wane, they returned to their normal methods of getting through the day. They ate out of their pockets rather than off a table, they climbed out of the windows rather than use the stairs, they threw mud instead of drawing and sewing. The team became more interested. Everybody was filmed all over again.

When six o'clock came and the team was still at work, the producer turned to Donald and said:

"Could you give us another day? There's so much material here, I'd like to double the length of the film. We've hardly started on the outside shots yet."

VERILY ANDERSON:
Beware of Children (Rupert Hart-Davis, 1958)

164

*TOWARDS A THERMONUCLEAR REACTOR*****

When the design of Zeta I was begun in 1954, there were reasonable grounds for hoping that temperatures would be produced which would give rise to detectable thermonuclear reactions. It was hoped further that if successful the information obtained would be sufficient to enable a bigger machine to be built. In effect, therefore, Zeta I represented a frontal attack on the problem of producing high temperatures in heavy hydrogen gas during a long enough time to establish that a thermonuclear reactor was possible.

In order that this should be done it was necessary that heavy hydrogen should be broken down into electrically charged particles (not in itself difficult); that these particles should be accelerated to high energies by electrical forces; and that they should be held for long enough in a confined space to enable their individual motions and energies to be randomly distributed and for energy-releasing collisions to take place. Because the particles are electrically charged, their movement gives rise to magnetic forces, while magnetic forces are used in turn to control their movement. There is thus a complicated situation—the result of mutually interacting, and changing, factors. This is inherent in the problem, and there were those—notably in the United States—who maintained from the beginning that the correct course was to concentrate on finding out as much as possible about what happened in a variety of conditions that might be relevant. This is the approach that would be followed in the normal way by a scientist, uninfluenced by practical objectives. But it is still arguable—when such an objective exists—that one approach, thought to be favourable, should be pressed harder than others.

"Zeta to Icse" from *The Times* of 23rd July, 1959

165

*THE SWING OF FASHION****

In the past fashions often lasted, with only minor variations, over several decades, sometimes much longer, like the wide-spreading skirt which was in favour from the sixteenth to the end of the eighteenth century. For men fashion is still in many ways remarkably constant. The lounge suit, for example, has altered the cut of the jacket, the shape of the lapels, the width and creasing of the trousers, but in all essentials it is the same dress today as was worn in the eighties. It would, however, be unsafe to argue from this conservatism in dress that men are by nature more stable than women and less responsive to suggestion: they are eager to buy mechanical razors which do not shave, shaving creams which do not lather, and fancy fountain-pens whose purpose must be to maintain social prestige, for they write no better, and often worse, than the old-fashioned kind. Women candidly seek novelty in dress, and not only do designers bring in for them 'new' colours and materials, new 'ideas' and decorations, three or four times a year, but radical changes may be made in the total appearance half a dozen times in a decade. Between the two world wars the skirt has been worn, for both day and evening wear, to fall above the knee, below the knee, half-way to the foot, to the ankle and to the floor, and at one time it was high in front and low behind. The waist line, in 1915–16 fixed just under the breasts, by 1922 had dropped so low that it crossed the thighs rather than the hips. The silhouette, seen from the front, has been bounded by straight lines, giving the woman the look of a cardboard box perched on two sticks; and at other times the silhouette has been more richly and naturally curved. Hair has been cropped to look like a man's, cropped over the nape, draped in a fringe over the forehead, piled up into a bang, hung loose over the eyes, hung loose down the back, worn in a net at the back, in a roll at the back, or round the crown, in a chignon, in a top-knot, in clusters of curls arranged in various ways. Hats have varied in size from a six-inch to a three-foot diameter. All these are only a few of the more noticeable variations in the appearance of women in the course of twenty years.

JOHN BROPHY:
Body and Soul (Harrap, 1948)

166

*THE EFFECTS OF ROAD TRANSPORT ON ENGLISH TOWNS—I**

The density created at certain places by the railways has been thinned out by the motor car. For whereas a goods train and a passenger train have a prescribed stopping place on the line, lorries or private cars can stop anywhere along a road. They can start at any time and stop at any place. There is no trouble with waiting at junctions, with changing from one line to another. The motor lorry, by[1] providing a cheap, rapid method of transport, altered the plan of most of the English towns. Light industry, that is to say industry which is not confined to a certain district, has moved from the congested towns of the North of England and the Midlands, to main roads outside London and the big ports, or to the outskirts of the town whose[2] centre it originally occupied. Stretches of pylons and forests of poles have brought electric power out to the country so that it is possible for a factory to be built on almost any site. Where[3] is it more natural to build a modern factory than beside a main road? For here is a broad route, provided by the State, for lorries which can leave the factory at any time for any destination. Buses and private cars can bring visitors from far greater distances[4] than in the constricted days of railways.

JOHN BETJEMAN:
English Cities and Small Towns (Collins, 1943)

[1] § **410**. 2.
[2] § **207**. *Note* (*b*).
[3] For "where" say "what place"; modify the sentence accordingly.
[4] Say "places much further away."

167

*THE EFFECTS OF ROAD TRANSPORT ON ENGLISH TOWNS—II**

The sons of the silk-hatted first-class travellers and even those of the second-class travellers on the old steam trains, could buy private cars before this war. They all have the Englishman's love of the country. In their new-found freedom they used to rush to the country and crowded every accessible town and village with clusters of semi-rural communities extending over a greater area by far than that occupied by the original town. Speculative builders, eager to save themselves the expense of building roads and drains and bringing power to country districts, built villas along the main roads where surface and light and drainage and power were already available. So the roads came into their own again and ribbon development, that most natural development, was the direct result of the motor car. Transport determined the plan and towns spread outwards until[1] they nearly touched one another. Coaching towns on main roads came once more into their own. The old inn in the market square was taken over by a combine and re-furbished in a half-timber style, vaguely reminiscent of a few hundred years before it was built: the stable became a garage: the market square became a car park: tea rooms opened in the main street; the old shop fronts disappeared as[2] lorries brought the mass-produced shop fittings, advertisements, films, signs, petrol pumps, magazines, multiple stores, the Morris's,[3] Fords, Daimlers, buses and chars-à-banc brought the people. On first glance, many towns came to look like a London suburb.

JOHN BETJEMAN:
English Cities and Small Towns (Collins, 1943)

[1] *A tel point que.* [2] *Comme? Lorsque? A mesure que?*
[3] Say, "and as the Morris's" etc.

168

*IMPRESSIONS OF AN INDUSTRIAL AREA**

The last twenty miles I did in a car—twenty miles of almost continuous squalor. The sun which had been shining all day from a cloudless sky disappeared behind a pall of smoke; the land was flat as a pancake and ranged along the riverbank were cranes, derricks and railway sheds; chimneys belched smoke; factories and mills were surrounded by acres[1] of squalid yard; the road ran through miles[1] of streets lined with little, mean houses, houses which were covered with a coat of grime. No single building distinguished itself, by reason either of its size or its beauty, from the mean monotony[2] of the prevailing architecture. As the car penetrated deeper into this district, my heart sank. The contrast between what had been[3] during the preceding seven days, between what had been even today in the places where man had largely left God's work alone, and between the places in which he had substituted his own, would have depressed anybody but a saint or a local inhabitant, for—and here we come to the point of all this—the local inhabitants did not at all share my horror. In the Town Hall there was a reception. There were the Mayor and the Corporation; there were smartly dressed men, noisy with heartiness,[4] beaming with jollity and agog for speeches. I had not expected this. At least, I had not expected 'this' to be quite so grand and I was not dressed for it. In point of fact, I was still wearing the clothes in which I had been walking in the Lakes, a pair of flannel 'bags,' stained, an old coat, torn, an Aertex shirt whose natural brownness could not wholly conceal its acquired dirt, and nailed boots. As I came stumping into the hall, I was made all too consciously aware of the deficiencies of my costume. I could see the company, so sleek, so black, so neat and so glossy, looking covertly down its nose at me so stained, so torn, so dirty and so clumping.

C. E. M. Joad:

The Untutored Townsman's Invasion of the Country (Faber and Faber, 1946)

[1] "acres," "miles." Is the author seeking to convey measurements? If not, terms like *vastes, interminables,* etc. could be used.

[2] "mean monotony . . . architecture." Turn by a more concrete phrase, *e.g.*, "the featureless mass of mean buildings."

[3] "had been." Use a more personal phrase: "what I had seen (known)," etc.

[4] "with heartiness." Translate: "and hearty."

169

*THE BEAT GENERATION****

The central fact that orders our lives, just past the middle of the twentieth century, is the harnessing of nuclear energy. As the years pass, those directly associated with this great work become more and more remote from the rest of us. They live in self-contained communities, hygienic and glitteringly new. These innocent-seeming new towns have guards on the gates, and are surrounded by barbed wire; and this is necessary, because although the work upon ultimate and almost-ultimate deterrents that goes on in these places is, we are told, for the good of all humanity, it is equally for our good that our susceptibilities should be touched by it as little as possible.

Many of us are happy to pretend that these spots on our corporate skin simply are not there (as many Germans were incurious about the exact nature of those camps established in forests or on moors rather difficult of access, confident that whatever was done by a sternly benevolent government must be for the national good). We live in our boxes, go from them each day to smaller office-boxes, use eagerly the devices that make living easier and more mechanical, behave—or try to behave—as though our world had a late-Victorian stability, and our deepest trouble was that of Huxleyan doubts. Is there, indeed (the box-liver asks), anything else to be done?

To this question the art, and more particularly the conduct, of the Americans who call themselves the Beat Generation offers an answer. Since the past, these artists say, now appears meaningless and the future has passed utterly out of individual control, man must 'cut himself off from those values which have propped up his vision of himself as the hero of history.' Religion, ethics, the idea of progress, the institution of marriage: how can they appear anything but ridiculous, once you accept (as these artists do) the pursuit of immediate sensation as life's logical end in the nuclear age?

"The Moral Anarchists" from *The Times Literary Supplement* of 17th April, 1959

170

*AN AIR LINER TAKES OFF***

He stared at the back of the seat in front of him, a worn, tired little man wiping his glasses.

Behind him the door closed; the chief steward passed by him on his way to the flight deck, a sheaf of papers in his hand and carrying a black briefcase. The forward door closed behind him and the engines started one by one, deep, reassuring rumbles faintly heard as though from a great distance. Presently the cabin stirred beneath him. Mr Honey looked out of the window and saw the lights of the airport buildings pass him by as the aircraft moved down the ring road to the runway's end.

He never felt the machine leave the ground. At the runway's end she turned across the wind and cleared engines one by one; then before[1] Mr Honey realised what was happening the runway lights were sliding past his window in acceleration and presently they fell away below. It was the first time he had ever travelled in an aeroplane with modern sound-proofing and it took him by surprise, because he had expected to be warned for the take-off by a great burst of noise. But there was no such roar, and before he realised quite what was happening the airport was below and behind. Then there was nothing to be seen out of his window but a blackness that reflected his own face and everything in the brightly lit cabin.

He leaned back in his seat and relaxed, savouring the comfort. Presently the stewardess who was attending to the passengers at his end of the cabin came up the aisle, stopping by each passenger and saying a few words, helping to tuck away the safety belt, taking orders for meals upon a little pad. She came to Mr Honey presently, and said "I'm sure you'd like a little supper before[1] settling down, sir. What can I get you?" She told him what he could have.

He ordered a cup of coffee and a plate of sandwiches; she noted it.

NEVIL SHUTE:
No Highway (Heinemann, 1948)

[1] § 405.

171

*DEFENCE AND THE HYDROGEN BOMB*****

If in practice there is no difference between Conservative and Labour policy on possession of an independent deterrent, what about their views of the circumstances in which the use of nuclear weapons should be initiated? The 1958 Defence White Paper, in a paragraph which gave great impetus to the movement for unilateral nuclear disarmament, said: "The democratic nations will never start a war against Russia. But it must be well understood that, if Russia were to launch a major attack on them, even with conventional forces only, they would have to hit back with strategic nuclear weapons. In fact, the strategy of N.A.T.O. is based on the frank recognition that a full-scale Soviet attack could not be repelled without resort to a massive nuclear bombardment of the sources of power in Russia."

Critics pointed out at the time that since such action would involve suicide the statement probably did not mean what it said. Definitions of what constituted 'a major attack' would probably prove to be elastic in the event. Moreover, the 1958 statement is not in line with current N.A.T.O. policy. General

Norstad's strategy is to have shield forces capable of imposing a pause (during which the aggressor would have to weigh the cost of continuing his attack) on anything up to and including a major attack made with conventional weapons only. That is, a major conventional attack would not immediately unleash the west's strategic nuclear forces. But though the 1958 statement appears to be out of line, it has never been modified by the Conservatives.

Labour policy, as given by Mr Gaitskell at Workington in July, is that the initiation of the use of thermo-nuclear weapons "is a question of defence policy in N.A.T.O. which cannot be settled by us on our own, but only in discussion with our allies." Later he said on B.B.C. television that though he could not commit himself in opposition, he found it very difficult to see the circumstances in which we could possibly use nuclear weapons first. This is a more realistic answer than the Government's statement in the 1958 Defence White Paper, which was the doctrine of massive retaliation, though in fairness one ought to say that the Conservatives are probably less rigid now.

"Defence and the Hydrogen Bomb" from *The Times* of 24th September, 1959

172

*POWER IN TRADE UNIONS**

There have been men who have risen to leading positions in trade unions who have not possessed the correct balance[1] between the will to power and their belief in the cause. But they have exposed themselves. It is easy, however, to make excuses for them. It must[2] be difficult for men to eschew material benefits—comfortable living and all the luxuries one associates with high incomes—when they are there for the taking and when, as so often happens, the efforts the leaders put into their work bear little results or when the results are not appreciated by their members and they are subjected to constant criticism[3] for being reactionary, or out of touch with the workers, or fraternising too much with the employers. It must be difficult, too, because national trade-union leaders normally meet employers' representatives on the employers' ground and they learn from first-hand[4] experience how the 'other side' lives. They are required to move about in social groups that are totally different from the social group from which they[5] sprang and, what is more important perhaps than any other factor, they learn that the people they have traditionally regarded as their enemies are inherently decent people who are protecting their own interests in the same way as the trade unionists are protecting theirs. There should be little wonder that[6] the weaker leaders lose their sense of direction under such circumstances. The men who have been through it and yet have retained their feet firmly on the ground have been men of outstanding social integrity.

V. L. ALLEN:

Power in Trade Unions (Longmans, Green, 1954)

[1] Translate: "kept in . . . equilibrium." [2] § **94**. 2.
[3] A simple rendering may be obtained by using *reprocher* (dative of person, *de* + infin.).
[4] *i.e.*, "personal," "own." [5] Emphasise. See § **236**. 1. [6] § **379**.

173

*THE ENGLISH HOUSEWIFE**

She is the slave of cleanliness, cookery, and monotony. She knows that she is an amateur, but she does her best with shocking bad material and little money; she knows that she is no organiser; but she does not realise that she is one of millions of similar amateurs who support, instead of combining to abolish, the stupid tyranny of the kitchen. Some day a wife will press a button and food will shoot in from a communal kitchen;[1] she will press another and the remnants of the feast will disappear.

It is only the capacity which women have for suffering in silence and their instinctive inability to combine which have preserved the stupidities of the kitchen.

She can sense every mood of her husband. She knows at once when he is laboriously carrying a secret; when he is clumsily trying to hide anything. He,[2] on the other hand, is blind to those occasions when, watching him sitting so placidly after his exciting day, she longs to utter a loud scream and hit his bald head with[3] the nearest metal implement. She wishes at times that he was less fond of his home. He is becoming part of the unadventurous routine. Is there no excitement in life; no unexpectedness? It is also the anniversary of their wedding. He has forgotten. She says to him hopefully:

"George, what day is it today?"

"Thursday," he replies promptly, looking over the evening paper.

"Hullo," he adds, "what's up?"

"Don't speak to me!" she cries, and bursts into tears; which pains and horrifies him. An entirely comfortable world has been suddenly shattered for no reason whatsoever!

H. V. MORTON:

Blue Days at Sea (Methuen, 1932)

[1] "from a communal kitchen." Translate this phrase immediately after "food." "From"="come from." [2] § **234**. 2. [3] § **287**.

174

*DOUBLE CLAIM*****

The claim for a substantial wage increase and a forty-hour week, which is to be presented to the engineering employers today, is unique among post-war claims in that it comes at a time when the cost of living is stable. For more than a year there has been no significant change in the index of retail prices and there is reasonable hope that this stability will be maintained. This circumstance could be regarded as an opportunity for introducing some measure of reform into whatever settlement is reached rather than as an excuse for repeating the purely negative reply which has been common in the past. Stable prices are not necessarily a good reason for refusing a wage increase, any more than rising prices are always a good reason for granting an increase.

The engineering claim is always of vital importance because, affecting directly or indirectly more than three million workers, its result rapidly influences other large sections of industry. It is of special importance this year not only because of the unusual economic circumstances but also because many union leaders are known to be anxious to concentrate their effort on shortening the working week, making engineering their main pressure point in private industry while they make electricity supply their main pressure point in nationalised industry. Both higher wages and a shorter working week would raise labour costs, something which no employer ever welcomes. They will have to decide not only whether either is tolerable in present circumstances, but also which is the more undesirable.

The case against a shorter working week appears to be much the more convincing. All the available evidence suggests that most working men would rather have more money than more leisure. Overtime is sought after to such an extent that in some industries employers have to offer it in order to attract the labour they require. There is not even any reason to think that a shorter working week would result in fewer hours being worked, except in rare cases. In the main the result would be more hours paid at overtime rates, with an increase in all the abuses which excessive overtime encourages. Earnings would be increased just as much as by an increase in rates but in an unbalanced and socially undesirable way.

"Double Claim" from *The Times* of 28th September, 1959

175

*DAZZLE***

Not infrequently a driver will be dazzled by a glare of light from an approaching vehicle particularly if its headlamps, though dipped, are badly adjusted. The greatest difficulty[1] is experienced immediately after the glaring lights have passed, because the eyes take a little time to adjust themselves to the sudden reduction of light which follows. On such occasions the driver is advised to keep his temper and to control his natural impulse to retaliate by switching his headlights full on. He should[2] avoid looking straight at the approaching headlamps and should direct his eyes to the nearside of the road ahead, keeping a particular lookout for pedestrians and vehicles; he will then get some benefit from the illumination of the road by the approaching lights. He will, of course, use his own anti-dazzle device, but will not black himself out by running on side lamps only. He should slow down or stop (see Highway Code, para. 51), and as soon as the offending driver has passed he may switch on full headlamps to overcome the ensuing blackness. Finally, the driver should bear in mind that this evil of dazzle, whilst bad at times, is by no means continuous. He will find that, if he makes a practice of using his own anti-dazzle device as he approaches oncoming traffic, the same courtesy will, as a rule, be extended to him.

One of the most difficult problems which beset the night driver is found in built up areas where the street lighting is inferior. Frequently he finds that his view consists alternately of pools of light from street lamps, and of darkness where the street lighting fails to penetrate owing to lack of power or to obstruction by overhanging trees. He is advised to illuminate these pools of darkness by using his headlamps whenever he can do so without danger to other road users. Frequently, of course, this will be impossible owing to approaching traffic, and in this event he should drive on his dipped headlamps or pass-lamp at a speed suited to the conditions. It is dangerous to black out completely by driving on side lamps only.

Roadcraft (H.M.S.O., 1955)

[1] *i.e.*, "the most difficult moment." [2] § **83**. 4.

176

USING A GEIGER COUNTER[1]**

He stood for some minutes next to his desk, in total irresolution. Then he left the room and, instead of turning right to the exit, went along left to the labs. Here he selected a key off his ring and let himself in. The labs were clean, light and empty; everything was neatly put away, no experiment was going on, everyone had gone home. He went to a wall cupboard and took out a portable Geiger counter.[1] He could have had his choice of[2] several; the one he chose was an oldish model, a plain wooden box to look at, rather like the long wooden containers in which wine merchants send by post a single bottle of wine. It[3] was of polished wood, and larger and longer, but its proportions were the same. It was activated by a small electric battery concealed inside at one end. At the other, the wood was cut open to disclose a dial, on which were figures which would record the intensity of the radiations of any radio-active materials brought near to it. To make sure that it was in order he brought the box near to the small knob of lightly radio-active quartz kept in the labs for testing. It began to count: Clack, clack, clack. Like a very slow, old-fashioned clock. The dial changed in harmony with the clacks, stopping at a very low figure which he did not trouble to look at. He made an entry in the book near the door, relocked the door as he went out, and went towards the exit with the Geiger counter under his arm. As he reached the quadrangle, he stopped again, once more in obvious irresolution.

RAYMOND POSTGATE:
The Ledger is Kept (Michael Joseph, 1953)

[1] *un compteur de Geiger.* [2] See § **123**. 4.
[3] Make sure that there is no ambiguity in the translation.

177

*EARLY MORNING IN COVENT GARDEN MARKET**

Merely from[1] an instinctive notion of avoiding the tangle[2] of streets I had combed on the previous day, I allowed myself to cut through Covent Garden and generally work[3] parallel with the Strand. Men were shouting and heaving sacks and baskets; amid a crowd of them I stood and drank[4] several cups of hot, dark tea, saturated with sugar. The smell of vegetables, the shirt-sleeved porters looking more like farm labourers than any kind of urban worker, the gum-booted men who had come in by lorry from the mist-hung villages before London was awake, all helped to increase my sense of unreality. Where was I? A provincial from a smoky bricked-up place far away, who had repeatedly dipped himself in metropolitan culture till all but the core of his mind was dyed in it, searching the capital city for a Latin girl from[5] the impossibly distant mountains, drinking tea with this bunch of rustic Cockneys—and all this amid a sea of cabbage-stalks, with a foreign-looking sun already striking burningly down through the Diesel-soaked London sky. It was too much of a mix-up. *A kaleidoscope*, I thought, but the word was too old-fashioned; the kaleidoscope had been a popular toy in Victorian times, but the spectacle of perpetually self-renewing chaos, always seeking new combinations, is interesting only from[6] the outside. Now we were on the inside of the kaleidoscope, looking out; I knew what I wanted to see, but I had to find her first.

JOHN WAIN:

The Contenders (Macmillan, 1958)

[1] Translate: "prompted by." Change the position of the word translating "merely."

[2] i.e., "labyrinth."

[3] Translate: "follow (a) road(s)."

[4] Translate: "stopped to drink."

[5] "from": *i.e.*, "who came from."

[6] Translate: "seen from the outside."

178

*DETECTION IN THE MODERN WORLD***

The business of detection is dull, even duller than the stories of detection. There are rarely dramatic confrontations, rarely brilliant flashes of deduction which make complicated confusion[1] fall suddenly into an ordered pattern, rarely even cunning planning which leads to[2] tight-lipped men in mufti all converging stealthily upon a heavily-armed criminal in[3] a sordid café. It is far more like the ordinary work of a middle-rank bureaucrat rather pressed for time; a great deal of it consists of receiving, reading, and analysing a large number of typed or telephoned reports and documents, and issuing or confirming instructions to act upon them according to routine. Anything not entirely in one's ordinary sphere is dealt with professionally[4] by experts, also according to their routine. The proper information having been obtained, the resultant action is usually already clear to everybody, and requires no more than the usual notation on a piece of paper or instructions by telephone. The established phrases are somewhat different (Treasury officials do not receive minutes stating 'You will proceed . . .'), but the atmosphere is the same one of rather dull correctitude.

RAYMOND POSTGATE:

The Ledger is Kept (Michael Joseph, 1953)

[1] Use a more concrete expression in French, *e.g.*, "confused and complicated elements."

[2] Translate: "leads up to the moment when," etc.

[3] Use an explanatory word or phrase before the preposition.

[4] Translate: "is passed to experts who deal," etc.

179

THE ADVANTAGES OF GRID-REFERENCE[1]***

Map-references are used as a basis of large-scale local surveys of various kinds, and for keeping statistics and records. They are used by education authorities and housing authorities for reference to the sites of schools and houses. The Ministry of Health already accepts map-references as an adequate description of a site. The grid has for some time past been used for recording collecting-points for road transport, and by contractors for dumping material for road repairs. Scientific associations use it for annotating the results of study in the field, and also for giving the exact place of rendezvous for meetings in the countryside. A big taxi-firm using wireless communication gives directions by grid-reference to its cars on the road. The grid is valuable for the quick calculation of distance, and I have heard from one borough that it is specially useful in giving distances to the ambulance service. A man in charge over an enormous area of the maintenance of specialised machinery made by his firm needs references to keep his location-lists and also for sending out his engineers; but he and others ask for gridded half-inch maps. The Ordnance Survey have already begun work on a new half-inch series, with the grid.

The most obvious job for which I thought the grid might be useful was the policeman's; so I wrote a circular letter to the chief constables of nine counties in different parts of England. One had 'no observations to offer.' One was opposed to the use of the grid for the odd reason that it would waste time; he and another said it was unnecessary because their men knew their ground so well. But a grid-reference, however well you know the ground, saves time by avoiding verbal descriptions in talk and writing; and it is obvious that the higher a report goes in a police force the less detailed the local knowledge becomes. And the police of the other six counties do in fact use the grid for numerous purposes. One chief constable said that all ranks in his force are now trained to use it; he and others were truly enthusiastic.

HUMPHRY HOUSE:
All in Due Time (Rupert Hart-Davis, 1955)

[1] For the technical vocabulary used in this passage, students could usefully consult Alain Bargilliat's *Vocabulaire de Cartographie anglais-français, français-anglais* (Institut géographique national, 1944).

180

*THE SCHOLARSHIP BOY*****

Such a scholarship boy has lost some of the resilience and some of the vitality of his cousins who are still knocking about the streets. In an earlier generation, as one of the quicker-witted persons born into the working class, he would in all probability have had those wits developed in the jungle of the slums, where wit had to ally itself to energy and initiative. He plays little on the streets; he does not run round delivering newspapers; his sexual growth is perhaps delayed. He loses something of the gamin's resilience and carelessness, of his readiness to take a chance, of his perkiness and boldness, and he does not acquire the unconscious confidence of many a public-school-trained child of the middle-classes. He has been trained like a circus-horse, for scholarship winning.

As a result, when he comes to the end of the series of set-pieces, when he is at last put out to raise his eyes to a world of tangible and unaccommodating things, of elusive and disconcerting human beings, he finds himself with little inner momentum. The driving-belt hangs loosely, disconnected from the only machine it has so far served, the examination-passing machine. He finds difficulty in choosing a direction in a world where there is no longer a master to please, a toffee-apple at the end of each stage, a certificate, a place in the upper half of the assessable world. He is unhappy in a society which presents largely a picture of disorder, which is huge and sprawling, not limited, ordered and centrally-heated; in which the toffee-apples are not accurately given to those who work hardest nor even to the most intelligent: but in which disturbing imponderables like 'character,' 'pure luck,' 'ability to mix' and 'boldness' have a way of tipping the scales.

His condition is made worse because the whole trend of his previous training has made him care too much for marked and ticketed success. This world, too, cares much for recognisable success, but does not distribute it along the lines on which he has been trained to win it. He would be happier if he cared less, if he could blow the gaff for himself on the world's success values. But they too closely resemble the values of school; to reject them he would have first to escape the inner prison in which the school's tabulated rules for success have immured him.

He does not wish to accept the world's criterion—get on at any price (though he has an acute sense of the importance of money). But he has been equipped for hurdle-jumping; so he merely dreams of getting on, but somehow not in the world's way. He has neither the comforts of simply accepting the big world's values, nor the recompense of feeling firmly critical towards them.

RICHARD HOGGART:
The Uses of Literacy (Chatto and Windus, 1957)

INDEX OF AUTHORS

The numbers given in this index refer to the passages, not to the pages

INDEX TO PASSAGES

The numbers given in this index refer to the passages, not to the pages